WALLOON WRITERS REVIEW

Eighth Edition

An annual collection of poetry, short stories, creative writing and nature photography inspired by northern Michigan and the Upper Peninsula.

Walloon Writers Review Eighth Edition
©2023 Walloon Writers Review
Cover Photography: "After The Storm" ©Kelly Suzanne Kelley

All rights reserved.

Walloon Writers Review
P.O. Box 936
Petoskey, Michigan 49770
www.walloonwritersreview.com
For information: editor@walloonwriters.com
Founding Editor: Jennifer Huder
Associate Editor: Glen Young

*Walloon Writers Review Eighth Edition was co-edited by
Jennifer Huder and Glen Young*

ISBN: 979-8-218-17381-4
ISSN: 2572-9683

CONTENTS

INTRODUCTION

Last October, a friend and I concluded a larger adventure with a road trip across the width of the Upper Peninsula toward home.

From the moment we crossed the Menominee River, I recognized a calm that can only be appreciated at the close of days spent exploring. That our ramble ended under cover of a brilliant autumn sky, the stars blinking on and off overhead, only added to the gratitude.

Northern Michigan and the Upper Peninsula has this sway over us.

Whether it is the end of a road trip, the mystery of that first bend of a river outing, or the early footfalls that make up a memorable hike, there is awe in moving.

So it is that for this newest volume of *Walloon Writers Review, Eighth Edition*, we asked our contributors to consider this urge to explore; to show us in words and images what it means to light out for the territory even if that territory is nearby.

Their journeys—from boulder-strewn beaches to scrub-choked trails and many unmapped places in between—celebrate geographic as well as emotional treasure, plumbing a range of responses made more real through art. In the pages that follow, you can traverse the ways location becomes love; or how these fruits of exploration ripen, sometimes in worry and sometimes in wonder.

As in earlier editions, there are voices both familiar and new, just as there are places we've visited before, and those that we see for the first time. Give your attention to each in turn so that you might uncover some fresh understanding of the places you know or the places you hope to discover.

As always, thank you for sharing this experience with us and for supporting the good work of so many deserving writers and photographers.

Glen Young, *Associate Editor*

cyanocitta cristata

-after Claire Malroux "Grebe"

Katherine Roth

Agent of the Air, there in the maple crown,
where snow has melted to birth this green

Diving through sky,
screeching at neighbors,
part devil, part angel

You are everywhere—
the weathered trellis, roof of the old barn,
pear tree branch

Speak to me, I cannot see above the lilac hedge

Who cares for you or your forever mate
in this place of troubles,
once a forest, Ojibwa land,
now the backyard of America?

The world is no more proud or elegant
than your crest of black, of blue

Speak, for I am listening
to your gull-like cry,
I have no feathers and cannot know
the drift of wind that holds me

Notes to the Lake of the Clouds

Katherine Roth

Lake Superior shoreline,
will you welcome me, allow me
to walk your trails with my new boots

You with your thimbleberry meadows
waist high dinner plate leaves, still green berries
beside forests of old growth hemlock

Reishi mushrooms, mountain rivers
turn to waterfall
in this relentless flow of water to lake

Did you place the orange hawk weed
along the path to help me
forget the incessant mosquito

Time and time again I am asked
suffering or a song
do you care which one I choose

Climb the summit to the Lake of the Clouds
And that is all we see   clouds reflect clouds
must it always be

what's in the way is the way

Duck

Alpena Walk May 23, 2022

Jeremy Proehl

Two days in a row
I've flushed you
from the runoff
that crooks into the woods.

You've learned to fear me
and I've learned
to cross to the other side
of the road
as I walk by.

Shadow

Alpena Walk June 8, 2022

Jeremy Proehl

nesting
in the reedy scrim
of North Point Road

crossing
disappearing into
Little Harry's Hunt Club

shadow
among shadows
lost to the morning sunlight

I take another step forward

My Manistee ©2023 Kelly Suzanne Kelley

The Religion Of Snow

Gloria Klinger

"This is the true religion, the religion of snow."
  —from "Shoveling Snow with Buddha" by Billy Collins

Snow in April?
Do the birds summon it forth?
They quaver and call
first one, then another,
the answer louder than
the question.

In the hush of dark morning
theirs are the only voices,
singing call and response,
meditating and praying
in the only church they know,
in the cold hard religion of snow.

And then the sandhill crane once more
with startling volume in the morning chorus
raises the question from deep inside
his warm, southern soul,
"Is this really snow?"

Winter Landscape, Munising ©2023 Elizabeth J. Bates

Swamp Song

Monique Bova

Late May in The Pigeon
Mystical floating forest
Engorged and vibrating
With the heralding trills of spring's horny rumpus
Each fresh rush of regeneration races
Like delicious mud-scented love through my veins
From the sudden neon bursts of buds
A tangle of birdsong
Alluring in its frantic bid for acceptance
And here in the rippling under
The caddis cling
Against rain-swollen sweep of stream
Whose mud banks captured
The tiny triangular impresses
Of the fawn's tenuous crossing
And I too am tenuous
Knees sinking as I lean
Reaching garden soiled fingers
Through the chattering mirror
Toward another day's swamp marvel
A springtime flutter of internal wonder
That life would plant me here to bloom

Storming the Castle

Gloria Klinger

Clouds the color of Damson plums
are a mix of dash and zip
hammering their way to thunder
batting away the sun.
The village of beach dwellers fled
with umbrellas under arms,
hoodies zipped against the chill.
Even the gulls seem to cower
in a posse on the sand.
Waves rub the lip of shore
their foam churned to rust,
resisting the urge to plunder
sand castles abandoned to rain.

Chicago's name derives from ramps,
which have nothing to do with traffic

Elizabeth Kerlikowske

On the door step, bundled in plastic, a clutch of ramps.
Wild, a little like green onions, these are Walloon ramps.

Sydnee left this gift for kitchen experiments.
I'll try anything once, even early June ramps.

Rapunzel's father braved the witch's wall
to bring his pregnant bride rampion, moon ramps.

Their pungent smell's a frog-spawning lake
and a night of bullfrog's sighs, bassoon ramps.

A feather duster removed from muck like a sliver,
green leaves, white bulb, between—maroon: ramps.

Her creek floods again this year, skunk cabbage grabbing
the clearings pierced by the needy harpoon ramps.

I'll ask Betty Crocker for a recipe and surprise Sydnee
soon with a bottle of red wine and noon ramps.

Tributaries

Elizabeth Kerlikowske

Trout Creek is a yarn that meanders into the woods
cold as winter in shallow pools reflecting
a fingernail of moon. Rills gallop
near the green cup where cousins dip for spring-
fed refreshment, pillows of moss and pine smoke.
Leaves underfoot crunch in ragtime. The old
man of the woods camps at the bottom of Elmira
Hill. We've seen his brown chair near the blind.

The Boyne is a novel when spring snow
melts up on the power lines, when the deer
drift down for apples, semis downshift
on 131 and the worn coveralls of the forest
need mending. Feel the tension in the weeping
willow when the old man climbs to the top
of the power lines in his Red Wing shoes.

We beg him to come back but it's fall again
and he will not be with us through the winter. He shaves
his hills bald for our snow; we huddle in the pocket
of his sky gray cardigan. Our thin branch
calculates the depth of future drifts,
a tape measure of water that never freezes.

Secrets

David "DJ" Savarese

The lake
at dawn.

The sun eases its way onto the page.

The boats still,
stenciled.

The clouds
haphazardly crayoned
over patterned rows
of blue and mauve.

The water—
no mere
reflecting glass—
blurs colors
into gentle
hues
that spread
across the lake.

The trees crowd the shore
for a glimpse of the spectacle.

Adrift In Wonder ©2023 Taylor Keiser

Horizon Lines

Skip Renker

From this distance, sails are isosceles
triangles billowing in white—the sailboats
hanker for the horizon, where
protected harbor becomes

the great inscrutable lake. Weekend sailors
seldom cross that long straight line, essential
to geometry, so rare in nature,
but use the calculus of wind

and tiller to curb their risky urge,
turn about in slow sweeping arcs,
give in gracefully before going
too far, though their motions fail

to save some watchers on the bluffs
along the shore from contemplating
with a sinking fear the law that causes
every visible thing to disappear.

Soundings

Skip Renker

A woman hemming a dress
hears the undulating noises of
unseen geese, flying at twilight
beyond and above the leafless
trees of northern Michigan
in late November.

She wonders if their calls
have meaning in this
universe of signs and runes,
so often indecipherable,
of trackless clues, of words
that rarely lead to anything
like revelation, yet beneath

the sky's invisible seams
the geese stitch their way,
sounding one another
and the world, as if
beckoning, beckoning.
She pauses with poised needle
to look up and listen.

With Axe and Saw in Hemingway Country

Dan Dueweke

It started as a summer storm. A line of storms actually, and they came across Lake Michigan with an intensity that would wreak havoc on my wood lot and topple countless trees. From our porch, I could see the forest swaying and large branches breaking off and blowing across the two-track leading to our house. I knew that once it passed, I would have much work to do both at home and as a trail volunteer for the Little Traverse Conservancy.

The Conservancy manages many tracts of land in Northern Michigan, including several that border Horton(s) Creek, the setting for some of Ernest Hemingway's Nick Adams stories. To live in Charlevoix and hike those trails is to absorb the Hemingway lore from the early 20th century when the last of the old growth logging occurred. Hand logging it was, with muscle and sweat, axes and crosscut saws. Hemingway would have known the sound of a saw "singing" as it was pulled across a fallen tree and heard the impact of a distant axe as it echoed through the river valley where he fished for trout. Yet it was also an era of depleted forests littered with the slash left behind by those loggers as described in *The Last Good Country*.

It's been 100 years since Hemingway walked through these woods, and much of the cutover land is now second growth forest. Some of the tracts have been acquired by the Conservancy and preserved for the enjoyment of future generations. Hiking trails, some following old logging roads, wind through these properties and are occasionally blocked by storm-tossed limbs or deadfalls. It is after such violent weather events that I walk those trails with an axe, a crosscut saw, and a volunteer's spirit. I could use a chainsaw if I chose to, but Michigan's logging boom took place before their arrival, and those traditional tools just feel right as I walk along clearing the way forward.

Starting at the trailhead, I hike downhill toward Horton Creek passing an enormous grey and rotting stump. That silent sentinel is all that remains of an old growth pine, a reminder of what was once here. Today, evidence of the storm is everywhere. Limbs and small branches litter the trail and partially broken limbs hang high in the canopy waiting to fall with the next stiff breeze. My young daughter is with me and carries my axe as we saunter down the trail. Better to walk slowly, take in the natural beauty of the woods and hear birdsong as we go.

It is not long before we encounter our first deadfall of the morning. The big maple is across the trail, and there is no easy way around it. I drop my pack and turn to my daughter.

"What's the first thing we do?" I ask.

"Look up!" she says. "It's the loose limbs overhead that will kill you if they drop on your head."

"Good girl," I say, knowing that she's paid attention to my safety lessons on our hikes. Seeing no overhead hazards in the canopy, I make a plan for where to saw, where to stand, and how to remove a section of the tree with the fewest number of cuts. Though efficient, a crosscut is no match for the chainsaw when it comes to speed. We are in no hurry.

Dirt and mud cling to the tree from yesterday's storm and that grit has worked its way into the bark. It will dull my saw if not removed. I mark the spots where I intend to cut and let my daughter peel the bark with the axe while I attach the handles to the saw. Both the axe and saw are antiques and acquired locally. They date from the logging era but are now being put back to work after generations of hanging in a barn or over a mantle.

Placing my saw on the tree, we begin the back-and-forth motion we'll use to sever the wood. All crosscut saws have their teeth spaced along the arc of the blade, so we cut with a slight rocking motion to keep all teeth engaged on both the fore and back strokes. We're double bucking – —a trail crew of two – —but I could also imagine Nick Adams on the other end of the saw (or perhaps Littless) working with me as a team to keep the saw in motion. Each pull of the saw removes little ribbons of wood that old sawyers called "noodles" and are the sign of a sharp saw. Soon our boots are covered in this wood spaghetti, and I smell a moist fragrance above the cut. Each tree species has its own scent, with some like the red oak being quite pungent. I notice the cut, or "kerf" closing as the tree begins to sag and feel the saw starting to tighten. I drive a wedge into the kerf with the poll of my axe to hold it open and prevent the saw from binding. Zing, zing, zing......the saw teeth are "singing" while working their way through more than a hundred growth rings on a passage back in time to when this fallen tree had first sprouted from a seed. We complete the cuts and roll the log aside. *Clear to hike,* I think, then we take a cool drink of water and continue down the trail.

Up ahead I see a red pine, flat on the round. I choose to chop this one and spare my saw from the gummy pitch that will leak from the cut. Not many people chop wood these days, mostly using their axes to split firewood. I have taken the time to thin the "cheeks" of my axe and hone it shaving sharp. Each swing bites deep and rewards me with a new scent – that of the piney pitch oozing from the sapwood. Soon the pine is dispatched, and my daughter gathers the largest chips to place trailside as evidence of our work and so hikers will know that a chainsaw wasn't used.

Nearing the creek, we pause in a hemlock grove for lunch. The valley has sheltered these soft-needled trees, and none have fallen. I look out at the water and half expect to see a youngster in a big straw hat, pole in hand, fishing for trout. I see no one.

Day's end finds us back at the trailhead, leaving only wood chips, sawdust, and a cleared path as evidence of our passing through Hemingway country.

Planting Roses at Walloon?

Ralph James Savarese

You've spent most of your life
trying "to separate by pricking"—
that's what it means
to distinguish yourself. It pains!

But now you want only a bed
and the bandage of oblivion.
The self's a needle. How to dispose of it?
No body should ever be some.

Take the rose bush, for instance,
that petaled siren.
A mast won't save you because
your ear's inside the bloom.

Sunset On Walloon ©2023 Neil White

Barn Buzzard

Jeanne Blum Lesinski

Behind the farmhouse, down the drive
on a main beam of the fallen barn
tripped by roots

                            –a neglected elm
against the field stone foundation–

the buzzard suns himself, wings wide
in the early afternoon heat of July.

Facing west he sniffs and surveys
the almost ripe hay field.

                           Hisssss.

He turns, observes us, aging siblings,
tanned and graying and mottled like him,

reinvesting in this familial place,
and our kinship

                  after long years,
riding air currents elsewhere.

Goldenrod ©2023 Katie Gray

Kayaking the Leland River

CJ Giroux

I idle in the channel's green gloss among patches
of poison: golden centers of water lilies

shine like suns that are safe to stare at.
Moving forward, following the disappearing map

of the kingfisher's deep *rat-rat-rattle,*
I find more danger and beauty—hosta, hydrangea, fox-

glove speckle the shore—but also stillness
under a willow's canopy, its branches curving

like the nave of a small stone chapel outside Sevilla.
I imagine inhaling lavender, its silvering leaves,

but both scent and touch remain at a remove,
so I head towards the village's old boathouse,

its eaves sagging and corrugated walls atilt;
there, I peer into yawning shadows until rain arrives.

In an empty slip in this manmade darkness,
my fingers run over roping as if reading Braille:

the message twisting, dipping, turning like a Möbius strip.
I seek Morse Code in the snare drum of the rusting roof.

Spider lace links beams—more threads I can't follow.
When I emerge into light, water slides

along the paddle's black handle, beads falling
on my wrists, arms in a misplaced benediction.

Instead of blessing myself, hand moving up, down, side to side,
making the sign of the cross as if at a funeral,

I just grip the paddle tighter. I edge towards
some other horizon I can't see, around the bend,

out of reach, following some invisible wake,
a series of crescent moons, elongating, never growing full.

Limbo: South of Leland, North of Beulah

CJ Giroux

In the kayaks that came with the cottage, my sister-in-law and I seek the point where the Whaleback's dorsal ridge slips into Lake Michigan. Sue paddles through shore water looking for petoskeys and blue slag to line her raised beds. I opt for land, a fraying beach towel laid over a lumpy mattress of rock. Though I don't expect sleep, I rest against driftwood, between bleached knot holes and cracks that begin, end without warning. In them I find scars and lifelines like those crossing wrists, palms.

Lake Michigan's surface is a cliché, smooth as glass, but I still want more clarity. South Manitou is hidden by haze, horizon, ocular migraine. To my left, beyond Good Harbor, but well before Beulah, the Dunes shimmer on their slant, like heat rash growing in August. And north by northeast, the moss-colored McMansion, which is the end of my morning walk and always out of reach, is hidden by white pines that jut upward. These jagged lines recall uneven teeth; the gaps between them; poor Yorick's lower jaw, separated from its mate.

Her arrival heralded by the slide, chime of stone against stone, Sue begins beachcombing. She returns bearing a crumpled Coors can from Indiana, brown beach glass, a faded tee (its sleeve torn) featuring Daffy Duck. <u>She</u> tells of makeshift fire pits and skeletons—a beheaded fawn or fox. Maybe a coyote she says, her own devil's advocate. As coconut sunblock covers the tang of algae and alewives on my fingertips, I imagine, like icons on a lunar calendar, the curved rows of ribs, their edges smoothed and soothed by light and silt, waves and heat. Sun, sand, water, ashes—our goal for the week, I suggest. Our end too, Sue counters.

Elegy for My Childhood in Traverse City

Isabella Gross

arrested by
      the pliability
      of wood

penchant for tenderness
      roots under soil
      feel warmth

sunlight settling
      no choice
      but chlorophyll

generations of ferns
      curled and furled
      leafy empire

in my backyard
      firefly M&Ms
      green red blue orange

starlight's
      earthly cousin
      quick bodies

blackberries hacked
      down
      and regrown

prickly
        unshaven moss
        older than

dad
        stacks wood
        back there

tree cemetery
        under their noses
        a little insensitive

salamanders
        exotic homebodies
        where are you

on the food chain
        owls hawks
        noseeums dogman

your prey
        my cat
        still lives

I hope
        we make
        our way

to the waves
        rolling in
        petoskeys

to glimmer
        like beetles
        in the grass

the wind
        whistles
        like a ghost

inches
        of the coast
        lost

ask me
        for directions
        I can

lead you
        even now
        so long since

can't assume
        it's the same.
        It will tell me

how
        to follow.

Lumber

Isabella Gross

fallen tree
spread upon the white ground
      like an autopsied lung   all brachial
                    amputated
                    with careful hands
two hundred feet
      from the woodpile   the family grave

the lung of a giant   of a Paul Bunyan or his brother

missing its enormous twin
      its donor body   somewhere   perhaps still
                        walking
with half the capacity
      as before the accident

Maybe an inflating hot air balloon
as a replacement
      organ

      he wades through Lake Leelanau
            with just his eyes
and nose
      above the surface
      breaching to rest on the sand
              stones
           and still-smoldering
              beach fires

dreaming of giant women
to the lonely call of the late-night loons

Breaking Through ©2023 Caroline Helmstadt

Eagle and Loon

Ellen Schettling Whitehead

I am living between
the eagle and the loon
on a pristine lake
in Northern Michigan
with crystal clear waters
hemlock, pine, white birch
secluded hills
solitude

Eagle –

An eagle soars overhead
gliding on air currents
strong and courageous
predatory spirit
always circling, searching

Loon –

Below the loon sways
upon the water's surface
then diving into its depths
it searches for perch
holding its breath

Sometimes I am Eagle
soaring, proudly, soaring

Sometimes I am Loon
diving, steadfast, diving

diving
soaring
subsisting

I am Eagle

I am Loon

Loon 4 ©2023 Ellen Schettling Whitehead

A Wandering Mind

Hailey French

In the morning my responsibilities loiter over me, but I ignore those responsibilities, and in return I feel young and in love with life.

Not the kind of youth where I have jellybeans and anticipation stuffed in my pockets. More the kind of youth where I accidentally eat a watermelon seed, and the seed doesn't leave my stomach but instead grows roots and flourishes into a watermelon patch and all the people pay $5 for a melon, but then they complain and say, "$5 for a melon? That's ridiculous!" and I tell them it's a small price to pay for someone who has a watermelon patch growing in their stomach. And they pay me the $5 for their sunkissed melons, cutting them open and letting the juice run down their chins as they bite into the warm fruit, and then they proclaim it's the best watermelon they've ever tasted.

Each day I go down to the lake because when you're out on the lake all day and the scorching sun is frying your skin the same way you take your eggs, the only thing you'd die for is a juicy melon. So, the people come and pay me $5 for my stomach melons and gorge on them. You wouldn't think people would crave something so much, but I assure you that each day they come and each day they devour the fruit, sucking their fingers dry from the remaining juices. And each day I only allow one melon per person and the people try to bargain with me offering me diamonds and large houses for a second melon, but I tell them fair is fair and they can only have one.

Then one day when the lake is a wetter version of the sky, which reminds me vividly of the color in my childhood bedroom, and the people form a line the length of six marching bands, my watermelon patch runs dry. It simply disappears. The people can't believe it, but I'm relieved because I never asked for that kind of responsibility. So as the people mourn my stomach melons, I take a dip in the cool water. The sun scorches my skin when suddenly I crave a juicy melon. I see a stand on the edge of the beach and ask how much for one melon. The man says $6 which I think is pretty steep for someone who didn't have a watermelon patch growing in their stomach, but I pay him anyway and cut open the melon, letting the juice run down my chin and savoring the sweet taste on my fingers.

Suddenly I remember I have a deadline today and I chug a bitter lukewarm cup of coffee, snapping out of my youth.

How to Move Beneath a Tree Without Disturbing the Chickadee

Kate Allore

To my dearest Nova.
May there always be Chickadees for you to talk to.
~Grandma Kate

Allow your eyes to multiply.
Let them scatter throughout your body
like the Birch tree, the Aspen.
See everything—
see nothing.

Don't breathe,
but don't hold your breath.

Lower your shoulders,
relax your hands,
and become the moss beneath your feet.

Settle softly into your bones.
Let your skin become like the leaves,
swaying to the rhythm of Earth's hum.

Keep careful watch over your heart,
encourage it to settle
into your belly.

For if you don't, the heart
will reach out to grasp
the Chickadee,

to transform
their ephemeral
into her eternal.

Practice,

        practice,

                practice...

                    ...sitting upon the outstretched
                        arm of the Pine overhead,
                    Chickadee did not notice me.

Me, with feet of moss.

Me, with feather light breath.

Me,

        no longer human.

I Think I'll Call Her Mary

Kate Allore

St. John of the Cross wore dark glasses, Martha threw a good party—
Mary sat at the Lord's feet.
  —Opening line from the "Initiate" by Charles Simic

She sat on a green plastic bench
outside her little home perched
on the county line.

A scrappy black and white dog lay beside her,
tattered quilt covering them both.

I don't know her name,
I don't know how old her dog was.

I don't know how many people
she had helped that day
or if she had made her bed.

There were no grand gestures,
no Ceremonial garb,
no Sacred Fire.

Just two upturned faces,
The woman and her dog,
peaceful;

receiving the simple gift
of a mid-winter sun.
Just sitting.

It was everything.
It was nothing.
It was enough.

Kids Creek Pathway ©2023 Carol Ritter

Fish Tale: An Elegy

Ellen Lord

How my body arched ---
his lure finding
its way in silky shadow
to pierce my lip,
his filament taut and urgent
--- and I rose
beyond the surging cascade
of thunderous waterfall ---
a quiver
of salmon colored dazzle,
glorious in the mist.

Seasonal Angst

Ellen Lord

I get so scattered,
could not recall the word amethyst
and it's my favorite semi-precious stone.
It took hours, then just dropped in
like a belated guest. I worry
about mental decline, like that helps.
I float about this quiet house, find comfort
in mindless chores, then pause ---
to gaze into the dormant forest.
Traces of feral friends wend pristine snow.
I hear crows, wonder why they never sound peaceful ---
then soften when an eagle spirals in full soar.
Mercy comes gently today, nature's reprieve
from chatter in my mind. I linger
by the window to watch. Wait.
It seems like ---
I can never get enough sky.

Cross Village

Katie Koziara

1.

The hunting rifle that shot Father John Bernard Weikamp's horse sits in the crypt, alongside the priest's body. Jurek felt sinful keeping it. A plaque marks the date of death: March 19, 1889.

Killing the horse was an act of grace. The speckled mare's left eye had grown cloudy. It stared blankly at the Catholic Brothers and Sisters whenever they traipsed through the pasture.

Jurek never had much drive to hunt in the Northern Michigan woods. On one occasion, he spotted a brown bear padding along the path ahead of him. He lined up, peering at the bear over the end of the barrel, but then lowered his aim. The bear moved farther down the trail, and Jurek turned back to the convent.

Jurek didn't miss the responsibility of the gun, but he did miss tracing the smooth grooves of the russet-stained wood with his finger. He preferred this form of meditation over praying the rosary. As Jurek puts on his cassock, he can still feel the patch of tender skin on his left shoulder where the strap of the gun rubbed against him all those years. He felt more authority then, watching black squirrels scramble up pine trees on his walks in the woods, than he does today, standing behind the pulpit, targeting the hearts of parishioners.

Jurek enters the sanctuary and walks toward the alter, to minister to those who live at the sprawling Benevolent, Charitable, and Religious Society of St. Francis. They are gathered for daily prayer, the brothers and sisters separated by a partition down the center aisle. From his heightened vantage point, he can see them both. There are less gathered here today than there were when they looked to Father Weikamp for wisdom.

He looks beyond them, beyond the crucifix that decorates the window, out toward Sturgeon Bay.

2.

It is the last Sunday in August 1879. Jurek walks in a pair of his pa's boots, a parting gift. He travels away from his home toward his new position at a Catholic community where he has heard young men can learn blacksmithing and woodworking. He considers it a step toward adventure and away from the life he is sure will bore him.

The footsteps he leaves in the dirt are closer together than they should be for a boy his age. His ma says she is convinced he'll hit a growth spurt, but he has trouble believing her words are anything but a kind lie.

Through a thick forest of trees, he sees the deep blue waters of Lake Michigan, a familiar sight. While this is as far north as he's ever been, he knows he would have gotten here eventually with a logging team.

Years ago, when he told his pa he wanted to try his hand at working on a ship, his father snorted, grabbed the family's crosscut saw, and walked him and his older brother out of the house and into the woods. The boys worked in tandem for hours, building up a sweat felling his first tree with the misery whip. He resolved right then to number his days as a lumberjack, and to number his days stuck in the community that no one seemed to escape for long.

Last month, when his ma suggested one of the boys propose to their neighbor, Marta, he decided it was time to pack his things.

He stops to tend to a blister on his left ankle, watching the white caps form along the waves. It's his second stop of the day. During his first break, he had napped in a bed of waning trillium, waking when he smelled smoke. He investigated and found a woman standing next to her cabin, smiling at him as she scraped the hide of a fox strung up next to the fire.

That night, as he sleeps on the floor of a stranger's home in Good Hart, he feels the fox tail brush his nose every time a draft creeps through the wood siding.

3.

The ritual of Holy Communion begins long before the pews are filled. He rises an hour earlier than usual this morning, though this will become habit soon. His Rite of Ordination is complete. Jurek's shoulders are narrower than Father Weikamp's, and the new priest has to pull his sleeves back up his arms as he cuts the Eucharist into pieces. What remains is a pile of small bites for the masses, enough to inspire hunger but not to satisfy. When he places the gifts in the tabernacle, he repents for his lack of contentment.

At mass, as the deacon reads from the last pages of the Gospel of John, Jurek looks out the back window toward the icy blue waters of the bay. A small black speck floats on the water, and Jurek thinks it's dirt on the glass pane until he realizes it is moving slightly to the east. It could be a freighter bound for Cleveland, or perhaps the locks on the St. Lawrence. It may be carrying lumber or iron. No doubt there is a large crew onboard, making their way somewhere different from where they've always been. It slips behind the son of God's pierced side.

"Jurek."

The deacon and the parish are looking at him. He has missed his cue to begin the homily. He walks over to the pulpit slowly, keeping his eyes fixed on the oak planks beneath him. His face flushes as he continues with the agenda, taking the flock through the prayer over the gifts, the Lord's Prayer, the Sign of Peace.

"Take," he says. "Eat. This is my body, which is broken for you."

4.

A few months after arriving at the convent, Jurek stands on the shore of Sturgeon Bay. The other boys take advantage of the calm fall day, skipping rocks toward the horizon. Jurek sits on a piece of driftwood, legs tucked into his chest, chin resting on his knees. Back home, his brothers are probably preparing for the salmon run. He wonders if Marta is married yet.

There are still several hours of daylight left, but the evening is already closing in on him.

"You are different than the others your age."

Father Weikamp's deep voice calls out to him. Jurek turns and watches the Father make his way down the path to the beach.

"I don't quite fit in with them," Jurek admits, scooting over to make space for the Father.

"You have something they do not." The priest forgoes the offer and walks toward the long grass growing on the dunes. "A curiosity." He bends the blades under his palm before allowing them to snap back into place.

Jurek turns his face back to the grey waters. Several waves crash into the shore before the Father speaks again.

"They don't question what I say from the pulpit."

"I want to believe, Father."

"He is a rewarder of those who diligently seek Him."

"I want to believe that as well."

Father Weikamp uproots a piece of grass and walks over to Jurek, laying it on the driftwood where the boy had made room for the priest. "You will take over this place when I die."

Jurek fears he has misheard.

"I am not fit!"

The priest shrugs and begins walking back toward the convent.

Jurek runs after him and spins the Father around by his shoulder. The Father stumbles a bit on the sand but smiles as he regains his balance.

Jurek places his palms together as if praying. "Please, choose someone else!"

The Father calls out to the boys splashing along the lake. "Come, follow us. It's time to eat."

5.

Milk sloshes over the lip of the pail he sets down next to the shed. He's never seen anyone enter the structure, though it's set just a few dozen yards away from the church. A crucifix sitting atop the peaked roof nearly doubles the height of the building.

The door is locked, but he peers through the window. Inside, a rectangular pit sits in the center of the small dirt floor. Bones fill the place where earth should be.

"How peculiar," Jurek remarks, then remembers he's supposed to be practicing the spiritual discipline of silence. He curses.

"Why peculiar?"

Jurek has seen Father Weikamp at mass every morning since he arrived last month, but he has never been this close to the priest. In person, the Father looms even larger, and the way he is standing eclipses the mid-morning sun. It appears his skin is on fire where his outline meets the sky.

"I'm sorry, Father," Jurek says, though he isn't sure why he is apologizing.

"Where do you think we go when we die, Jurek?"

It is news to Jurek that the Father knows him by name. He is just one person among hundreds at the complex.

"Heaven," Jurek says.

"The soul, yes. But the body?" Father Weikamp gestures toward the pile of bones. "I spend hours here each morning, praying and meditating."

Jurek feels the Father is inviting him into some secret. "Why?"

"To remind myself how fragile all this is." Father Weikamp sweeps his arm to point to the acres of dry grass, the large boarding houses, the school, the church. He places his palm on his heart. "And this, too. When you accept that, Jurek, that's when you can begin living."

He steps around Jurek and enters the crypt. Jurek watches him through the window as he kneels at the altar. Jurek wonders why, if life is as fragile as the Father says, the man wastes so much time in a shed.

6.

For nine years, the Father frees Jurek of daily chores. He spends his days shadowing Father Weikamp, reading the sacred texts, and praying. The others don't feel he is worthy to lead the convent one day, and Jurek agrees.

This morning after mass, Father Weikamp arrives at the stable, Jurek in tow.

"Disease is spreading in Middle Village," the priest says. "I'm going to see how I can help."

He approaches his beloved mare from the right side so the horse can see him coming. She extends her long neck toward the Father, allows him to rub her patchy side. A brother assigned to stable duty begins hoisting a dark leather saddle atop the animal, but the Father takes the harness himself and places it lightly on his mare. She braces as he pulls himself onto her back.

Jurek rarely gets permission to leave the convent's grounds, and he aches to go on an adventure. "Would you like me to accompany you, Father?"

"One of us should stay close in case we're needed here." The Father exits the stable and turns south.

Jurek crunches his lips together, trying to hide his disappointment, and reaches for his rifle. It hangs on a peg nailed into the wood sides of the barn, and though he doesn't keep close watch over it, no one else dares touch it. The rest of the monks understand that the rifle is a gift from the Father, who sees hunting as a way for Jurek to confront death. It was clear Jurek wouldn't take to daily meditations in the crypt.

Jurek spends his afternoon walking the woods. He thinks about God. He thinks about life. He thinks about death. He fails to pull the trigger on an unsuspecting animal. He comes to conclusions he's not sure Father Weikamp would appreciate.

7.

Confession is Jurek's least favorite part of the day. He hears the same phrases he has heard again and again. Forgive me, Father, for I have sinned. A woman yells at her children in a moment of exhaustion. A man cannot stay faithful to his wife. Jurek passes out Our Fathers and Hail Marys, ashamed he cannot give them something more that will free them from their troubles. Privately, he makes his own confession: He cannot rid himself of the feeling that he, too, is doing something wrong.

In his best dreams, he is a builder. He is a miner. He sells ale in a pub. He sells pastries on Main Street. He is no longer a service provider. He offers something to the masses that can be counted, can be packaged, can be held.

In his dream last night, he arrived at heaven's gates. Father Weikamp sat atop a stone pedestal, his legs crossed under his white vestment. The Father's hands were empty, palms out. His eyes were not the dark black orbs they were in life. Instead, two cloudy pearls sat in his sockets, looking past Jurek.

"Father, is it you?"

The Father did not look at him.

"Father?"

The Father kept looking beyond him.

"Father!"

The sound of his own voice woke him up. He rose immediately, rushing the few paces to the dresser in his barren room. In the second drawer, he felt for the vestment, and in his haste accidentally ripped one of the crocheted lace crosses one of the nuns had sewn into the design. He sat on the ground, wiping the snot under his nose with the cloth.

8.

Jurek is meditating, gun strapped over his shoulder. He should be in the woods, but he is drawn to the water today instead. He has been sitting so still that a fox has joined him, his feet making tracks in the snow just a few dozen yards away.

Jurek studies the fox, then sees its ears perk up. It takes a moment before Jurek picks up on the sound, before he hears the steady pattern of a horse approaching. He turns to the tree line behind him.

Father Weikamp and his mare appear through the pines. At the water's edge, there are no trees for Jurek to hide behind. Instead, he pulls out his gun and aims it at the fox, as if he has been hunting the whole time.

The move startles the fox, who runs away from Jurek and toward the woods. The bottom of its tale brushes against the mare's back leg as it runs for safety.

The horse bucks, tossing Father Weikamp off her back. His foot catches in the stirrup, and he cries out once for help as he falls to the ground headfirst. The mare gallops toward the safety of the water, dragging the Father along with her. He is silent as his body makes a path in the snow, parallel to the mare's trail.

Jurek cocks his rifle, aims at the horse in the distance, and pulls the trigger. The horse brays and tries to continue toward the water despite the metal in her chest. She drops just shy of the shoreline, bringing the Father's final afternoon ride to a close.

He runs to the Father, whose legs are pinned under the horse's body, arms reaching out as if toward opposite ends of earth. His lips are slightly parted, but they are not moving like when he quietly reads the *Secreto* during mass. The crimson-dyed snow around his skull begins to melt.

Jurek sinks to his knees on the pebble-strewn beach, closes the Father's eyelids, and looks up.

9.

After the first mass, Jurek walks to the lake. His snowshoes keep his body from sinking into the deep powder. He does not think of the chill until a piece of snow drops off a pine bough and lands at the nape of his neck. He tries to shake it off, but it melts too quickly. Icy droplets travel down his back.

He could turn around, but he doesn't want to return to the church yet, disappointing Father Weikamp with his lack of discipline in this daily meditation practice.

A cardinal flits in and out of view up ahead. When he reaches the point where the path opens up to the beach, the bird sits waiting for him on a high branch, perhaps to watch over him, perhaps to watch his next move.

He opens his coat, reaches in his pocket, and pulls out the pastie he took from the mess hall on his way out the door. He holds it in his hands for a moment, letting the heat warm his fingers. As he unwraps the butcher paper, the scent of cooked carrots and potatoes and pork finds its way to his nose. He tears off a piece of the pastry's seam and tosses this crust a few feet ahead of him. The red bird descends to earth to enjoy the feast.

British Landing ©2023 Sara Wright

Presence

James Bogan

The dinghy tied to the mooring ball
implies the departed sloop
bound across crinkled Lake Huron

Allied to a small breeze
the absent boat has already
slid beyond sight
south through the suspended gate

Piling up over Lake Michigan
the all but impossible clouds
shimmer orange and cumulate
into billows

with one touch
the mute witness
brackets
the moment

The Crack in the Island

James Bogan

looks more like a ditch
lined with dead leaves
though geologists testify to
profound back-breaking fracture.

What they do not tell us
is that the Crack is really
the entrance to the Fudge Mines
at the base of the Island's existence.

The tidal power
of the Full Moon
opens the fissure
for the exchange
of magma-boiled fudge
in return for
raw sugar.

Untold tons
are shipped off monthly
from Maniboajo Bay
in lateen rigged Feluccas
—fudge ballasted—
and bound for Nubian shores.

The East Bluff

Philip Rice

What has come to pass by
this island? What lights have drifted
along the glossy waters, up
the edge of our smaller world?

An orb rises—is it Saturn or Sirius?
Someone, quick, check the internet—
no, it's just Jupiter (of course, how
could we forget) and now a great floating
body—a beautiful boat comes around the bend—
somebody, quick, look at the radar, where is
the Pearl Mist headed in all her shining
splendor which surely gives Venus a run for her hard-
earned money—ah yes, of course, to Sault Ste. Marie,
where else?

And what was the name of that poet, you know, the
one who wrote so beautifully about silence and
summer? Can somebody please look it up? I can't
recall her name. I guess all poets have written
about those things. I'll think of it later.
It will come to me.

By the way,
Whatever became of asking the stars about our fate
without ever knowing their names—whatever became,

after all,
of naming the stars to begin with?
Whatever became of sailing into the mist, toward
the edge of a bigger world, not knowing if you
would ever arrive, let alone return?

Wandering Out

Philip Rice

So you wander out
in search of Whitman's "splendid silent"
away from the child's barking laughter,
away from the carriage driver's shouts,
away from the father's patience worn thin,
away from the mother's patience gone,
away from the furious merchant,
the endless chime of the cash register,
the clatter of dropped luggage, the clang of crashed bicycles,

You wander out and find the damselflies perched on marsh
reeds,
You are hypnotized by the song of cicadas, their perennial horny
hymn,
You gaze up at the turkey grass and long to touch its seven-foot-
tall fronds,
You commune with the ducks, the bumblebees, the cabbage
butterfly,
you caress the milkweed.

You listen carefully.

Behind it all, and within it, whatever
it is, the distant
noise of engines—
oppressive, inescapable

Albany Shipwreck ©2023 Lindsay Way

Sailing to Mackinac

The Port Huron to Mackinac Yacht Race

Mono D'Angelo

As a veteran Great Lakes sailor for over forty-five years, I have raced in the prestigious Port Huron to Mackinac Yacht Race multiple times. I am not an "old goat" (someone with twenty-five consecutive races to their credit), but I've competed enough times to know "The Mackinac" is a physical and mental challenge.

The race has been sponsored by Bayview Yacht Club ninety-eight times. Long considered the premier yacht-racing event on the Great Lakes, this race is between two hundred and sixty-five to three hundred miles long, depending on what course is sailed. Most yachts choose the traditional course, which sails north to Georgian Bay then turns left on a westerly heading to Mackinac Island. The race can be one of ideal conditions or a "what am I doing here?" kind of moment. The 1986 Regatta was one such race.

Aboard the 33-foot yacht, *Jazzy*, were seven men who have all sailed this race before. My friend Jerry owned her, and he assembled a strong crew with four helmsmen, including myself. One of the most difficult jobs in this long-distance event is steering the boat. It takes total concentration to stay focused, something not easy to do, so we switched drivers every four hours to keep us on course. We would live aboard *Jazzy* for about three days in very cramped quarters. *Jazzy*, a J105, was a good size boat as far as Mackinac boats go. It was solid, had a roomy cockpit and was very fast in the right conditions. Jerry's responsibility was to assemble seven men who he knew who could endure the rigors of this race without confrontations with one another.

The race is demanding. You don't sleep well, often times you can't eat because it's too rough. After twenty-four to thirty-six hours, you sometimes cannot tell whether you are sleeping or awake while lying in your bunk. Sleep deprivation begins to play tricks on your mind, and most sailors get a dose of it along with fatigue at one point or another.

The hardest physical condition to overcome is sea sickness. Lake Huron is capable of waves over eleven feet, and many racers have succumbed to Huron's dark side. The best way to combat it is stay topside…spend as little time as possible in the cabin. Most of the *Jazzy* crew had experienced sea sickness at one point in their sailing careers and had developed a natural resistance to it.

Equally important to avoiding getting sick is rest and nutrition. Fatigue spawns bad decisions if conditions deteriorate, and bad decisions can be dangerous.

"The Mackinac" has often been referred to as the race between the two best parties of the summer. Port Huron hosts the fleet on the days leading up to the race. Several hundred boats are docked on the Black River preparing for the race, and the Friday night before race day attracts thousands of spectators to Port Huron's River Walk. Each boat displays their colorful "battle flags" and a collection of award flags from previous races. There are bands, pubs, and excitement that builds toward the start parade on the next day.

By 10:00 AM Saturday morning, the fleet casts off and slowly makes their way down the river and out to the starting area located just north of the Blue Water Bridge. We started in warm, muggy conditions, with light winds and the chance of thunderstorms. There's an old sailing axiom that says, "the race doesn't start until the sun goes down." The *Jazzy* crew prepared for the most challenging aspect of The Mackinac…night sailing.

Each man layered warm clothes under their foul weather gear. Keeping warm is as essential as keeping fed. Nighttime July temperatures in the middle of Lake Huron frequently drop into the fifties from daytime highs in the seventies, and each crewman wears a safety harness or life jacket at night, no exceptions.

The high cumulus clouds at sunset forewarned us of impending severe weather. The race committee also radioed storm warnings to the fleet, confirming what we had already observed. After the last light of day had vanished, the lake was as black as the night sky above. There were no stars or a moon to light the way. Heat lightning could be seen on the western horizon as the squall lines rumbled toward us. The thunder soon could be heard well before the powerful streaks of lightning could be seen rattling across the sky. The breeze suddenly dropped from ten knots to zero, and we waited for the storm's arrival. Each man handles this moment his own way, but all experience some degree of anxiety. If you sail, you've been in storms before, and the crew was prepared and professional. There was no panic, just an organized readiness to drop sails upon the helmsman's command.

It wasn't long before the squall line could be heard roaring across the lake toward the fleet. Sounding more like a low-flying airliner, the brunt of the storm brought forty to fifty knot winds across *Jazzy's* beam. As the first wave of wind and rain hit us, the force of the wind rolled *Jazzy* over at about a 40-degree angle. The helmsman screamed out, "Be sure you clip on your safety harness and keep one hand for the boat," as he maneuvered the stern directly into the heavy air. By now, the rain was accompanied by stinging hail and bolts of lightning. The strikes illuminated the darkness for miles around with an unnerving randomness. *Jazzy* escaped being struck, but all boats were not as fortunate. In what felt like forever, the lightning storm was over in minutes.

The spectacle of a storm over open water has few comparisons. There are no buildings, trees, or mountains to hide behind. On a sailboat, there is no outrunning a storm. But when the boat and crew are prepared, mid-summer thunderstorms are an accepted part of the experience. Nevertheless, I am always in awe at the power of these storms and hold a special respect for them on Lake Huron.

Fortunately, these summer storms only last about 20 to 30 minutes, and after this one passed, the weather forecast indicated we should not see any more storms. Once the crew resumed their positions, the skipper yelled, "Hoist the big kite and a staysail. Looks like a big beam reach for the rest of the night. This is our air, so let's power her up." We resumed racing *Jazzy* hard again and sailed on towards the Cove Island Light, the halfway point of the race.

We rounded Cove Island Light about noon on Sunday, and the weather forecasts held up. The improving weather was perfect for sailing this time of the year. As we headed west, one hundred and twenty miles from the finish line, the wind shifted to the northeast, allowing us to fly our spinnaker dead down wind. The heading put us directly on the rhumb line. The wind freshened, and the crew pushed *Jazzy* for every ounce of speed she had.

The sun had warmed up the day, and a sixteen-knot breeze had *Jazzy* aggressively slicing through the royal blue waters just south of Drummond Island. The telltale hiss of a spitting wake off the stern was all that could be heard for hours. As night again began to fall, we knew it would be very different from our previous night.

Once the sun faded away, we could see stars for the first time—lots of stars. Only in the absence of any artificial light can the magnificence of the night sky be truly visible. We were fifty miles from any point of land, and there were no clouds. As the night wore on, millions if not billions of stars appear in every direction. Shooting stars and even a portion of the Milky Way Galaxy were visible to the naked eye. The stars illuminated the lake surface, casting a sparkling reflection atop the slow rolling motion of the water. The visibility was almost like daylight conditions, with clear views to the horizon. We could also see some of our competitors sailing a similar course.

On the eastern horizon, an orange/red glow was observed just below the horizon. It continued growing in intensity. It was 2:00 AM, and the crew gave a quiet cheer to welcome the moon passing through the Earth's horizon. As it finally cleared, the glow became a fiery red sphere, hanging behind us like some weird kind of intergalactic lantern. This phenomenon was not new to the crew, but the appearance of a red moon is always welcomed as a good omen.

Some of the sleeping crew below had heard the commotion topside and climbed up on deck. While the moon continued to rise, the lake took on a surreal reddish orange glow for as far as we could see. The size of the moon seemed enormous as it changed from red to its more natural grey/white tone. Even a few craters on its surface were visible to the naked eye. It is natural events such as the blood moon and an eternity of stars and distant galaxies that makes this race worth the price of admission.

As we approached time to change watch, the entire crew was now on deck. The boat was still sailing very fast in almost perfect sea conditions, and our privileged view of northern Lake Huron at night was worth losing some sleep over. No one wanted to go to below and miss such a superb sailing experience. So, we all stayed awake and sailed *Jazzy* through a night like most people never get to see.

It was my turn to take the helm, and things settled down. Some of the crew went below and the rest of us sailed the boat. Helming a boat at night is challenging since there are no landmarks to reference. Because I steer using a specific star to help stay on course, I spent a lot of time looking skyward. We were about seventy-five miles east of Mackinac in the widest part of Lake Huron when a once in a lifetime event in my sailing career occurred.

Just forward of the starboard beam were some unidentifiable lights. At night, strange lights can be deceiving and are always treated with caution since their location cannot be determined. I was fixated on the lights, and as we closed the distance, they took on a lime-green tint and were swirling in all directions at the same time. Then it suddenly became clear…*Jazzy* had sailed into an Aurora Borealis, or Northern Lights as some people like to call them. The beautiful light danced all around our position. I recall feeling a little intimidated by this rare event although I never knew why. It seemed as if they could be touched, but of course there was nothing to feel. I was so distracted, I began steering erratically until the phenomenon vanished as mysteriously as it appeared.

Each time I compete in the Mackinac, I'm reminded what a unique destination Mackinac Island is. It's as if Mackinac was frozen in time. Motor vehicles are not allowed. Instead, horse and wagons move people, luggage, and cargo off of the ferry boats and to their final stop. Rich in historical artifacts, the island is a living piece of Michigan's path to statehood. And it's also wildly popular for its quaint charm. And of course, there are plenty of pubs and eateries to entertain the thousand sailors that invade Mackinac every July.

After finishing the race on a Monday afternoon, we cleaned up the boat and headed for the showers. After hot showers, the grass-covered hill adjacent to the harbor was covered with dozens of sailors enjoying a well-deserved nap on solid ground. With the fleet safely in harbor, the party was on. On board cocktail parties were in full swing. Dozens of different songs were blasting away as guests and spectators mingle with crews from all over Michigan. After a few hours of celebration, hundreds of sailors make their way to Mission Point to join in the summer's best post-race party…the awards ceremony. Free drinks and the thrill of collecting hard-won trophies topped the list of celebrations that make the Mac Race the premier sailing regatta on the Great Lakes.

Eventually, however, all the race boats have to return to their home port. The weather forecast for the next forty-eight hours called for fair conditions on the lake, and we decided to get going early to take full advantage of the comfortable seas. We departed Mackinac harbor on Tuesday morning under clear skies and light breezes.

The three crew members aboard *Jazzy* were all friends, and this transit felt more like "a boy's night out." The ship was well stocked with food, a few beers, extra fuel, and a loud stereo. As predicted, the weather was chamber-of-commerce, tourist video perfect. The only downside to the ideal weather, however, was light winds, flat water, and not much sailing. We had a hundred and forty-mile journey before us and knew this majestic lake could be a fickle lady when it came to sailing, so we continued motoring a good distance offshore hoping to find some wind.

At the upper reaches of Lake Huron, the Michigan coastline resembles an untamed wilderness. There are miles of nothing but pine trees and rock-covered beaches. Occasionally, the smoke of a distant campfire or the sweet pine scent of the forest would drift far out onto the lake. Such aromas five miles offshore are more like a spiritual moment for me. I found myself wondering how many ancient mariners must have had similar voyages a hundred years earlier. I felt a strange sense of camaraderie to the Chippewa and Huron warriors who first canoed out on to *Karegnondi,* the ancient's name for Lake Huron.

I was on late watch about 2:30 AM Wednesday morning. The twitching autopilot and chugging diesel were the only sounds to be heard. We moved steadily south at hull speed, passing Rogers City and Alpena to the west. A quarter moon began to blush the eastern horizon. It began as a bright reddish crescent, its pointed tip piercing the black lake edge, and then quickly ascending into the night sky. The resulting soft, grey glow illuminated Huron's gentle waves as thousands of starburst reflections swayed with the rhythm of the swells.

About five-thirty AM, the sun began to gently color the eastern edges of the ebony-hued heavens in a pink tint. There were clusters of low hanging clouds on the horizon that quickly picked up echoes of the vibrant glow, exploding in colors of tangerine, crimson, and bronze. Some of the sky was cloudless, and the black-lined horizon soon gleamed in a bright, copper colored patina. As the sun inched skyward, the colors blossomed in a vibrant urgency. The cloud formations altered shapes from fluffy to towering and majestic. The sky became a living pallet of dynamic motion, with the intense colors soon reflecting off the glazed surface of the freshwater ocean.

The horizon vanished into a water-colored collage, resulting in a living, pulsing canvas of churning clouds and red orange beams of sunlight. After the sun erupted above the edge of the world, razor-edged shards of pulsing color pierced the dawn like the unpredictable brush strokes of a Dali masterpiece.

Someone once said we get twenty-five thousand sunrises in our lifetime, give or take a few. Although the cold nights on Huron left me chilled and tired, I felt especially lucky to have been on watch to witness that morning's visual artistry. And by the way, *Jazzy* finished second in our class.

The Wet Crow

James Lenfestey

All night rain carpet-bombed hungry leaflets,
plashed glass, drummed rooftops
like a persistent distant Memorial Day parade.
At dawn downspouts dripped regular as a clock
to the mournful stride of an ore boat
through the Straits toward dying Indiana.

The bell buoy clangs once every swell,
the horizon a closed circuit of gray
as we asleep upstairs, garden half in, half out.

A wet crow struts the glistening asphalt road,
step, neck, step, neck, step, neck and peck
between black feet at what is left in wet.
And what is found. Step, neck, step, neck,
and peck.

Homo Homini Lupus

James Lenfestey

In college I fell in love
with Georges Rouault,
his pseudo-stained glass
impasto like cathedral
stained glass windows,
especially one image:
a lone hanged man
in a landscape of
savagery and fire,
the inscription:
"homo homini lupus,"
Man is wolf to man.

Now that I am old, I've learned the wolf
a better friend to man than most, the
good it does cleaning up our mess,
damaged deer devouring forest browse
like plagues of dustbowl locusts.

And I now see the clear-cut
that was my path, behind me a swath
of trampled grass and homeless "game,"
that childish word for wild life
one eats if one can solve their riddles
chronically wasting the brains of all of us.

And I have heard the chorus of the wolf
at home in wild woods over the horizon
as the sun sets, a polyphonic orchestra.
I howled back my thin note of longing,
desperate facsimile, inviting the pack
into the glow of the fire at my camp
to ward off the terrible predators
of my kind.

Rivers Are The Rest of Us
Barbeau, 1974

Glen Young

From here I wonder if you remember that old
rail bridge, not so high above the dark Charlotte
near where it bleeds into the mucky St. Mary's,
no more than a short mile as the gulls fly
from the single story almost-shotgun shack
that was the summertime we could not
get enough of. Remember that first moon shot?

You ever wonder if that river still bends the old
way, drifting smoke-like below the old park,
next to the rotted tracks, those high banks
shadowed with white pine and switchgrass,
or the way afternoons curled around the sun,
freighters in the distance stealing the current,
with pike tight to clumsy lines trolled over
the canoe's dinged gunwales, or how we lay
in the unmowed grass, putting up hoppers
or running from snakes only warming
with others atop the old wood pile, and how
it smelled of mud and goldenrod, spiders
in the windows or along the bathroom floor
and the dream that we could go on so long
as the river kept running and we never looked
back to where the others had gone inside?

Presque Isle River, Porcupine Mountain State Park ©2023 Elizabeth J. B

Fish Rock

Milton J. Bates

They arrive in ones and twos.
A herring gull is first to find
the fish remains on a sandstone slab
sloping into Lake Superior.

It pipes a shrill cry to friends,
but the signal is intercepted
by a pair of eagles that drive
the gull away and help themselves.

The eagles fly off when they've had
their fill, leaving the scraps for
disgruntled gulls and late-arriving
ravens to quarrel over.

We are last to dine. Our table is
set, the wine poured, the salad tossed.
Two trout filets, seasoned and breaded,
come hot from frying pan to plate.

There is enough for all, both birds
and bird watchers. None of us doubts,
except the gulls, that he or she
got the best of this morning's catch.

Salamander Nights

Milton J. Bates

What was all the fuss about,
he wondered, that drizzly
April night in Presque Isle Park.

So much commotion and noise,
so many restless bodies
on the wide asphalt river.

Though stiff from cold and blinded
by flashlights, he stayed on course
over pavement and snow-crust

to the party at the bog. How
they would admire his sky-blue
spots, his midnight-colored skin.

Pike on Peshekee

K. Matthew Springfield

There's an old family story
Of how our grandparents met
One summer in college
Out west of Marquette

Along the banks of a river
Where luck turns to fortune
But fortunate men
Rarely know at the time

That day started off, just like any other
Slept in too late, but his guilt would soon fade
Well, the Peshekee River, it ain't much to take
In from the grade, just like any old stream

But he knew a good spot, like countless before him
Where the waters ran deeper, and the fish liked to swim
So, he hiked up and down, through the tall Jack Pine stands
Till a voice he did hear, faint on the wind

So soft and sweet, floating o'er the boughs
Calling him to the river, calling him down
There in that place, she looked up in greeting
A smile, then a wave, and she finished her song

She looked so familiar; he asked if they'd met
"Now we have," she replied, "my name's Yvette"
He rested a minute. Pretended to need it
Regarded the river, and the country so fair

Then she heaved up her rod, it bent in a shudder
Whipping around, whistling through the dry air
Wasting no time, she moved like the lightning
Her voice echoed like thunder – "it's a big one, I think!"

She fought like a thief, on three days of hunger
Her curses were flying, and so was the fish
With her hair in her eyes, rose gold in the sunlight
Matching the tall grass in the hot summertime
She fought like a thief, after three days of hunger
The waters left riven, and their hearts skipped a beat

Well, that pike was long gone, they'd cooked it for supper
Fried up cakes with breadcrumbs, picked out any bones
That was a long time, 50 years at least past
But her song made him smile to himself faintly still

They'd gone back to that spot, every year on that same day
The third time he'd asked her, what's that shining right there?
Now he went by himself, never needed a map
Their spot on Peshekee, left to him now, alone

She fought like a thief, on three days of hunger
Her curses were flying, and so was the fish
With her hair in her eyes, rose gold in the sunlight
Matching the tall grass in the hot summertime
She fought like a thief, after three days of hunger
The waters were riven, and their hearts shared one beat

Here and now settled in, he stopped listening and looking
Till the world all around him, ceased to exist
With a flick of his wrist, he sent the line screaming
Plastic lure disturbing, then retrieved from, downstream

The third what did it, somethin' saw what it liked
It twisted and turned, jumped, "Oh! It's a pike"
A pike on the line, always made his pulse flutter
And a familiar song rose, up deep from his heart

He fought like a thief, on three days of hunger
The waters were riven, and his heart skipped a beat
Before the net came, it made one last effort
It flew through the air, like a rocket that's failed

Well, it tumbled and crashed, at the foot of the river
In a tiny rock house, that the river had built
It'd cut through the line, and now looked right up at him
One eye at a time, waiting on his next move

Only one move to make, he inched towards the edge
Just barely in reach, it had one last move too
The pike lunged for his hand, and held on real tight
So, he twisted and spun, flung it out of his sight

Whatever became of, that old Northern giant
He'd never find out; would've hoped it survived
Peshekee was warm, though he felt not a splash
Its waters were low now, and his head the rocks dashed

He'd slipped on the bank, at the foot of the river
And a familiar song rose, up deep from his heart
There in a memory, she looked down a grinnin'
A smile then a wave, and they finished her song

She fought like a thief, on three days of hunger
Her curses were flying, and so was the fish
With her hair in her eyes, rose gold in the sunlight

Matching the tall grass in the hot summertime
Fought like a thief, after three days of hunger
But the waters lay calm now, and their hearts did not beat

The Curve

alongside the border between Michigan and Wisconsin

Raymond Luczak

The railroad tracks careened by Montreal River,
its rusty dust sprinkling the dandelions
when trains north from Chicago and Milwaukee
barged through like fat ladies. With what,
I had wondered. But I never learned.

Grasses flapped cowlicks as I picked curs
off my athletic socks. Sparrows swooped lines
crisscrossing the silent tracks as the breeze
slowed down into a horse's steady trot.
I checked my nose and peeled off some sunburn.

Pebbles crowded under the large slivers
of six-by-sixes while strawberry vines
slithered away. I watched out for bees,
tiny helicopters roving for a better plot
of a more giving nectar beyond the ferns.

The shifting sunlight made branches quiver
as I walked further away from telephone lines.
The sun pounced on my face out of the trees.
The drainage pipe for the pond was now clotted
under the tracks, now a steep curve.

A sharp wind rushed through me. I shivered
a little as I pulled up a half-dry log beside
the tracks. But it made a crooked see-
saw, rolling back down with a plop.
Paddling turtles fled with lightning swerves.

The velvet heads of cattails knocked each other
like dominoes as I peered down into the shine
of the pond's surface. It stayed black-green,
mirroring only the dragonflies. I sought
to discern something beyond mysterious blurs.

After I'd climbed the bank, I felt that tremor
with my feet. The train couldn't be far behind.
I leaped off the tracks, I bent my knees,
I closed my eyes, I knew enough not
to look up. Pebbles pelted my shoulders.

I clutched onto the earth's low quivers
until the train's full length had gone by.
As I stared at its last car, I breathed more freely.
Pebbles tumbled out of my bowl haircut as I thought
how much I'd give to steer that mad curve.

Greenwood Reservoir

Carol Ritter

I followed my husband's broad back up the steep side of the island, carrying only some snacks and drinks in a daypack. This island on Greenwood Reservoir looked so very charming as we approached it in our little boat, a peak of granite and green rising out of the lake like a Northwoods volcano. The land around it had long ago been flooded out by the construction of a dam on the middle branch of the Escanaba River for the benefit of a mining company. The forest floor disappeared beneath the rising waters of its mother river. The old Escanaba would not recognize her old neighborhood now. The low spots of cedar, the mounds of high ground, the thick leaf litter, all now submerged in tea-colored water.

I wonder how quickly the water rose to consume the land when the downstream dam was constructed by hoards of men, backhoes, and cement trucks. Was the river choked off bit by bit until some final concrete blocks went into place? Or was the dam built alongside the river and an alternate path excavated? Until one day when the old river was suffocated by dump trucks loads of dirt, until it cried "Uncle!", gave up the ghost, and fled into the new, raw channel, seeming more hospitable despite the blockage of the dam. At some point a compromise was reached where the water accepted its only exit into the free world. So, the flooding was inevitable and the terrain agreed to yield. The muskrats kept moving to higher ground. The squirrels had to abandon their favorite trees as water started to rise around the trunks. Deeper and deeper. It must have taken a long time for all those trees to die, as their roots gasped for oxygen. Their trunks turned green under the water and the fuzzy murk of what had been their leaves and needles became a playground for young fish. The elder fish must have been utterly confused as their simple highway of life became a vast forest of decaying lumber. They must have wandered far to the east and far to the west of their old, well-worn channel, exploring dimensions never known before. Puzzled, dumbstruck, mouths opening and shutting in amazement as the linear world of an ever-moving river became more of a mysterious ocean, growing deeper every day. By the time the tallest trees were submerged, the fish remembered no other life. Walleyes replaced rainbow trout, bluegill gangs took over the weedy edges. And powerboats tooled along on weekends, ferrying picnickers and tent campers to new terrain: tiny, picturesque islands of Northwoods beauty.

From the North Shore

Sheryl Greene

Yesterday's storm tempted us here
to the water's edge, where,
eyes squinting against the high albedo glare,
my sister performs the alasana squat-shuffle,
seeking lightning-sintered fulgurite,
fossilized chain coral,
or the translucent bands of big lake agates
newly strewn across the swash zone.

Ripples wash over my sky blue water shoes,
over my small pale hands, palms down,
shifting layers of wave-worn pebbles sluiced bright and sparkling
in the spring sun.
Rising, I whoop and dart across the sand,
bucket swinging,
scattering seagulls into flight,
then breathless, stoop over my sister's towel display,
a geological collection,
carefully selected,
arranged in neat rows.
She frowns, having left her serious scrutiny
to peer into my empty bucket.

My fists open, fingers unfurl
exposing the winged shape of a sun-bleached bird pelvis
and a flat black skipping stone.

I slide the bird bone into her front pocket,
murmur "fragile treasure"
and slip away
to sling my skipping stone
at the hazy line between water and sky.

Hugginin Cove, Isle Royale 2022

Jennifer Uehlein Reynolds

My sleepy brain registered the snap of twigs and muffled crunch of lichen. The sounds came at predictable intervals, every few seconds, a gentle plodding. Then a snort. As my mind cleared, I peered through my hammock's bug net, under the edge of my rain tarp. In the pre-dawn twilight, my eyes struggled to focus. The sounds of movement came again, and a silhouette emerged: four spindly legs moving parallel to the tree trunks. I scooted a little lower in my hammock and saw the whole animal: a bull moose grazing the vegetation around our campsite. It was so close that I could hear it chewing and the inhale and exhale of its breath.

My two backpacking buddies were still asleep in their tents, gently snoring and murmuring every so often. Should I try to wake them? How, without startling the moose, which was way too close according to the safety guidelines described at the orientation by the park rangers?

"Robin! Nicole! Wake up! There's a moose in our campsite!" I hissed. They continued to sleep, while the moose turned its head in my direction, then resumed grazing. I chose to simply experience the moment, rather than continuing to try to wake my friends, watching this huge creature amble around, eating, occasionally tilting its head to free its ridiculously giant antlers from a branch or vine.

I began to hear more steps from the hill above our campsite—another moose was making its way toward us. Again, the spindly legs were the first thing that came into my view, as a cow moose meandered down the path, stopping near where I had tied my hiking shoes to a tree branch to dry out beyond the reach of mischievous foxes. My companions still slept as the cow moose began to forage, stepping between my hammock and their tents.

I lay back in my hammock, watching through the gap between my hammock edge and rain tarp as the two moose continued to roam along, chewing, sometimes grunting, as though in pleasure eating or maybe as a warning to each other not to crowd their space. I was caught in a sublime moment of exhilaration, seeing these massive creatures in this breath-taking landscape, wondering if I was a fool for entering their world, feeling small in the presence of their size and strength.

As the moose gradually moved away from camp, down toward Hugginin Cove, I dozed back off to sleep, and when I later woke to the full sunrise, it seemed the encounter had been a beautiful yet somewhat terrifying dream.

Moose ©2023 Jennifer Uehlein Reynolds

Little Wondrous

Robert Vivian

How glad of heart to be skipping stones of water words across a little lake in northern Michigan so precious dear I whisper *Wondrous* upon seeing it every secret and sacred time and the beating heart of a tucked away wildness I walk around with silent child awe taking me back to the first memory of water, which is pouring out of me even now so that I am human sluice gate and fervent praise running down a field to forever, little lake belonging only to loons and peepers and an astonishment come back again after the many waterfall years to bless me and anyone who comes to it out of a hushed and holy reverence and the luminosity of glowing leaves and flowers and ferns burning down to golden at the end of September so that they almost crackle in your fingertips, how deepening and quickening and well-springing of heart the dew fed moss on trails soft as an eyelash falling onto the sleeve of a cashmere sweater worn by the one you love and oceanic of heart, clarion of heart and magisterial of heart gone raining, gone weeping again the live long hours whose dappled lights settle lower in the sky as summer moves into autumn like elegy in the turning cold and metallic air and little lake, little wondrous and heart-shaped H20, little dwelling song of innermost and intimate feeling where the best part of me abides and is given room and summons to roam and to wander and how this lake poem must have a heron in it stepping highly and carefully as befits her matchless grace for the next fish and the next, the whole forest bejeweled and bedazzled by drops of water where a pilgrim can go and sip freely, how glad and steadfast and fervent of heart and I think I happen in waves and in the turning of the seasons for we are elemental after all, snow, fire, and ice and how before long the little lake will be frozen over and I will ski across it under a full moon as bright and stark as any stone lifted from a mountain, the susurrations of the skis the only sound, the whole forest leaning forward and listening as only trees can hear and hold the whole world for us even as they offer up their sacred breathing, and little lake, little page opening onto eternity in clear shallows I believe this pen and keyboard are willow branches teaching me how to bend and how to yield and how to weep in great heaving sobs whose reverberations are maybe meant to help the earth grow new flowers and trees and even birds who turn our sorrow and shame into bursts of bright upward flight on their way to soaring and the stars and the vast eternal joy that never ends.

The Forget-Me-Not Path ©2023 Moon Seagren

Shadow Bird

Edd Tury

*"The raven spread out its glossy wings
and departed like hope." —Cecilia Dart-Thornton*

A man rests on his porch
in the middle of the woods,
far from neighbors or asphalt.

A quiet time…
He loves quiet.
It stills his mind.
He longs to become part of the forest.

No sound but birds.
Mating season.
Alive, singing, spreading seed.
They remind him of songs he once sung,
when he was young and virile.

On the grass, dandelions prosper while
trees open their hands,
accepting the sun.

The birds grow quiet.

A black shape startles,
his muscles tense.

A raven clears the eaves.
He watches the bird follow its shadow.
Mythic bird, bird of prophecy, bird of life…of death.

The man stands and steps into the sun,
raises his arms out to his side and
slowly waves them up and down

making a shadow angel,
as the raven slips over the horizon.

Untitled Snapshot, Circa 1998

Stephen Hooper

Down on the linoleum with a freshly-unboxed Lego set
From the K-Mart that begat another Kohls
While parents and grandparents and great-grandparents visit,
droning, for hours
Rhubarb and raspberries growing alongside the old woodshed
Blue moon ice cream slowly melting on the table
What was in that upper room, I never really knew, and still do
not to this day
Then, loading up the minivan
Or maybe Grandpa's conversion van, "The Land Jet"
We'd head out to the old camp
Peering through the trees
The red-and-white check of the Big Boy graveyard caught my eye
Until one indeterminate year when I was older
It disappeared, like a phantom, or ghost ship
And that old steel bridge always did haunt me
Rusted over concrete cracking
One lane rusted steel truss
Shipped in pieces, from somewhere on the Allegheny upstream
of Pittsburgh
Could it support all the heavy hours of summer amblings?
No sooner did I worry when we had already crossed
Winding miles of asphalt, surrounding green from ground to
treetop
Until we reached the old camp, tucked up on a sandy, wooded
bank above the water

Oh yes, as soon as the sliding door flung open we were rushed
by hordes of hungry mosquitoes
But it didn't matter.

Craig Lake Sunrise ©2023 Stephen Hooper

Maxie and Her Camera

Suzi Banks Baum

"Not at least until summer," Mom calls up from the basement to answer Maxie's question. Mom wouldn't wear her clogs today, so Maxie wanted to. She digs through the basket of shoes and boots in the back hall, searching. It is a bright fall morning. The birds, who had gone quiet in the chilly wet days this week, are up early and singing. Maxie can wear Mom's clogs now since their feet are almost the same size.

"You are growing like a sunflower," Grandma Joan told her the other day.

With Mom's hollered approval, Maxie jams her stocking feet into the shoes and clops down the sidewalk. She is early for school and alone.

Maxie walks six blocks, down the alleys, to Holy Name High School football field. Early like this, bacon and coffee smells float out from the houses. Alleys are quiet places, cluttered with boats or snowmobiles on trailers. Open garage doors tint the air with the tang of gasoline and oil. Trash cans lean on back fences next to gates that lead to swing sets and garden patches in most yards.

Slipping through a slit in the fence around the football field, Maxie cuts across thick grass toward Third Avenue. Pretty much right away the heels of her socks get soaked. She'd planned to take them off before she got to school, but now she wants to ditch them in a trashcan. But she won't.

There are hardly any cars and no bikes out at this hour. She crosses Third Avenue to the gate of Lakeview Cemetery.

Maxie has an idea. She is one of the only freshman on the yearbook committee, which is run by Mary Jo Frossard, one of the smart kids from church. Mr. Rand, the faculty advisor is the hippie Junior and Senior year English teacher who assigns science fiction books. He talks with the kids about movies. Maxie thinks the committee kids are cool, but that is not why she wants to be there.

She wants to be a photographer. She has studied the kid who stalks the perimeter of the football field with the official yearbook camera, a 35mm, slung around his neck. She watches him turn the camera toward the cheerleaders, when they are exactly in the middle of a jump or stacked up in a pyramid, how the field lights halo their long hair. She can imagine what the pictures look like, the girls' breath chuffing out in the night-cold air. Grandma Joan's sister, Aunt Bug, teaches Maxie photography stuff when they are out on walks, how to do a thing called "framing a shot."

Taking pictures of people she doesn't know makes Maxie feel like a spy. But outside though? Maxie knows how to see stuff.

At the yearbook meeting yesterday, Maxie volunteered to take random outdoor pictures with her Kodak camera. It is only a pocket Instamatic, but the committee said they'd pay to develop her film. Since the committee will only use a few color photographs for the yearbook, she wants these to be really good.

The guard house at the cemetery gate is empty, so she hustles in. This place is run by the Catholic Church attached to Holy Name. Only plastic flowers are allowed. Clusters of colorful bouquets jut out from cement planters in front of old headstones. Some of the headstones are doubles with room enough to list the husband and the wife. A few stones are half empty, where only one of the couple has died. Maxie shivers when she passes these. "Creepy," she says to no one.

Maxie thinks that Lakeview is a ridiculous name for this cemetery. Even if all the dead people sat up and craned their necks to the east, they still couldn't see Lake Michigan. Even if all the trees between 19th street and the shore were chopped down. Escanaba sits on a high bluff above the lake. All they'd see if they sat up in their graves is sky. Besides, if they are dead, couldn't they float around and see whatever they want to see?

Maxie sets her bookbag on the dry headstone of the Wickström family. These must be from the family of the people who own the camera shop on Ludington Street. But these are really old Wickströms. They died in 1910 and 1920. She figures they won't mind her bag.

Maxie pulls her slim camera out from her sweatshirt pouch. She doesn't know what to do with her left eye while her right eye peers through the viewfinder. She's watched her parents screw up their faces when they take pictures of her and her sisters. Maxie tries to not scrunch up her face when she focuses on the maple trees in front of her.

This reminds her of what happened yesterday in Social Studies with bald Mr. Meyers. First off, bald Mr. Meyers lets the boys in class do whatever the heck they want to do. Tim Ball and Donny Oberg—two not cool boys she's known since her family moved here in 5th grade—were cracking themselves up during study hour. She had no clue why. But when she reached up to wipe the saliva from her upper lip, she realized they were mimicking her. How she licks her lip and tips her head when she reads. They rolled off their chairs laughing so hard. Mr. Meyers lifted his eyebrows at them without a word. Raising his eyebrows, which are the only hairy place on his head, shut them right up. The way they laughed made Maxie's tummy ache. Her shoulders squeezed up around her neck as she turned her back and kept reading.

Maxie isn't sure if her teacher has a sickness that makes him bald, or if he shaves his head to look like Kojak, because no way does Mr. Meyers look like that guy on TV.

Here in the cemetery, the sunbeams begin to touch the right side of the maple treetops. Maxie clicks her camera a few times. She shifts her stance like Aunt Bug taught her. You could watch the sun rise so quickly on the treetop like that. Right before she is ready to stop, a silent vee of geese cut across the sky over the maples, and she clicks a few more times. Maybe this roll would prove to the committee that she can handle the official yearbook camera. They could be sure she wouldn't waste film. She would practice how to sling the strap over her shoulder and draw the camera up to her eye to make a photograph.

But in this moment in the cemetery, the trees and the geese and that sunlight are just right for her. Maxie looks at the trees for one more minute, then sticks her camera back in her sweatshirt pouch and peels off her wet socks. She slides her cold feet back in the clogs and turns toward school. Even from three blocks away, down the flat avenue to the high school, she hears the early bell.

"Kind of disturbing for you dead people, eh?" she says to the old Wickström family stone. Maxie swings up her book bag and runs to the gate. She wants to make it to the cafeteria in time for a warm cinnamon bun and a carton of milk before first period.

She can smell the thick white frosting from here.

Fogust

Karen Nemecek

August did not dawn as much as fog
when she rolled over Presque Isle
and unfurled a damp grey blanket
all the way to Little Traverse Bay
to cover us until noon.

Here, closer to the North Pole
than the Equator,
we expected as much,
even chuckled at this cool taunt,
and dressed accordingly
in our morning ensemble,
namely: short pants and long sleeves.

Yet what heady superpower
we possess,
to biblically part
this partly cloudiness
loosely cinched at our waists,
by simply ambling
across tired grass
to deadhead shrub roses
or reseed spent bird feeders,
before stopping all forward
morning motion
to stand and contemplate
the hue of blue spruce,

all the while certain of the sun's contract
to strip misty sheets from the flowerbeds,
and her eternal promise of a warm kiss
on bare shoulders by two o'clock.

Roadside

Karen Nemecek

north of the Au Sable
summer's evergreen crush
hugs this sweet stretch
of interstate
where new blue decrees
duly direct me
to food, gas, and lodging

while faded painted verse
endures
roadside
among chatty aspens
or peeling birches
and lures
simple motorists
toward
wrecked ships
mystery spots
pictured rocks
and houses of light

Fogged Morning, Seney ©2023 Michael Sipkoski

Child Atop a Half Constructed
Root Beer Stand, Swamping Hot Tar

—after Theodore Roethke

Greg Rappleye

Sweat gluing my shorts to my skinny legs.
My Chuck Taylor shoes leaving the starry marks
of Chuck's sole across the tar-papered roof.
Three buckets of stinky hot tar staring up like accusers.
Six bags of pea gravel to be thrown across pools
of hot tar, once tar is poured and slopped and spread.
Windless, and no white clouds rushing anywhere.
Not far off, not far at all, a tangle of cedars shade trout
stalking *caddis* through the water-weeds
of a mystery river. A current I can almost hear
babbling below the desultory traffic.
And no one, no one I actually know pointing up
and shouting, "You're too close to that edge!
Watch out! For Chrissake, kid, don't fall!"

Elegy with Blue-Handled Filet Knife

—August 26, 1974

Greg Rappleye

The day she dropped me still bleeding
in Ann Arbor—fall semester, my duffel bag
jammed in back, we went to Drake's for cold limeade
and Mam bought a double to-go, because
she'd stashed a pint of *Mohawk* under the driver's
seat to brace her for the trip back north.
She knew I was never going back
to Da's orange-and-brown hot dog stand,
not after Monday night, when he slammed me
against the fryer over a spilled order of onion rings
and kept coming like a Kerry bull
because I was not worth a good-goddam
and I thought of the blue-handled filet knife
I'd slicked across a honing stone
just before the dinner rush, the blade
blood-warm in four inches of sudsy water
and pulled myself to the stainless-steel sink—
splash sizzling across the black grill—backing off
her snorting man, eyes wide, circling the prep table,
until an angel of a sane and better nature
whispered No, you're gone tomorrow
and three hundred miles south, over limeade
in the calm of Drake's Sandwich Shop
you'll hear her say she loves you, for the first time
in your pathetic life, if you stumble out the back door
now, hide all night in the jack pine woods
and do not stab her man.

Previously published in the Chestnut Review

Where Leaves Sound Just Like the Rain

Becky Serrano

In northern country,
when autumn breeze
whistles through tops of
brightly, tinted trees.
Rustling, dry leaves
sound just like the rain.

Fall winds swirl woodsmoke
in fair velvet sky.
Leaf-laden twigs dance.
From bowing branch fly.
Pitter-pat song, leaves
sound, just like the rain.

Stand still this moment.
Silent. At wood's edge.
Foliage whispers.
Mimics soft cloudburst.
Strain to spy raindrops.
Imagined. Or, real?

Fungal Bouquet ©2023 Taylor Keiser

The Upper Peninsula:
The Widower Explores His Heart

Linda Nemec Foster

His brother-in-law
knows all the strangers in town
he still lives alone.

More trees than people
more stars in the dark night sky
more silence than words.

Late summer colors
already bleed red in leaves
the woods are turning.

The coldest season
ice on Superior's shore
deep moans his heart hears.

How Lake Huron Paused
During the Seasons of Pandemic

Linda Nemec Foster

It started in winter: the long pause
of iced blue. A man gathers teal
for a face and counts bare branches.
Their natural separation becoming almost permanent.

> Becoming almost permanent, since spring
> was locked in the thin yellow
> of a concentric sun. As if a woman's heart
> was wound tight. Her face, a gray shadow.

> A gray shadow that mimics summer
> but gets lost. Is this how the world
> has been reduced? An unanswered question
> we ask ourselves in silence.

Our selves in silence, we begin autumn
or fall—as we still call it—
the season of falling away. A person's outline
on the lake's shore holding fast to stay, to remain. Alive.

Rayburn Estate Pines ©2023 Kimberly Ruley

The Dwarf

Edd Tury

When I regained consciousness, a dwarf, dressed in tattered camouflage overalls, was standing over me. I drifted in and out for what seemed to be hours, and each time I opened my eyes the dwarf was in the same spot. I tried to speak, but the small man put his finger to his lips, motioning me to be quiet. When finally I could keep my eyes open, I tried to evaluate my physical condition. I believed I was alive since I seemed to be aware of my surroundings and of the incredible pain in my leg and chest. As my mind cleared, I remembered what had happened and why I was lying on my back, severely injured. The dwarf made no sense.

I had set out (this morning?) to cut firewood. It was the early '80s, a time of high fuel costs, and I had installed a wood stove in my home. I already owned a pick-up truck and a chain saw, so I only had to add some muscle to heat my house. On this particular day I had neglected to tell my wife where I would be cutting. Felling trees in a forest alone is risky business, but back then I was still young enough not to worry about dying from a lack of critical thinking. Looking back, I wonder at the fool I was.

The morning was beautiful, late spring, leafing almost complete, the forest sun-dappled and cool. Dead elms were easy to spot, barkless and barren, their graying trunks apparent. Common wisdom has elm burning cold, not a choice firewood, but those of us who were twice warmed knew better. Dense enough, easy to find, abundant—who could ask more from a free resource?

I idled my truck along an old two-track and scanned the woods for the standing dead I could legally harvest. When I found several close together, I parked and prepared my chainsaw for the work at hand. I believe my problem started with the first one I cut. When the elm fell, the top wedged itself between two live trees, driving their supple trunks in opposite directions, creating huge opposing energies—like drawn bow limbs—vectors of death. They were squeezing my tree north and south, separated by several feet, a cocked ballista. The only thing holding the trunk back was the wooden hinge between the stump and the trunk. Of course I didn't recognize the trap. If I had, I would have cut the hinge from the other side. I am alive today because one needs to stand close to a tree to saw it. When the hinge let go, the trunk caught me midbody with insufficient velocity to kill me on the spot but enough to launch me backward in breathless surprise, a crumpled human catapult shot. In time I came to learn that I was 20 feet high at the top of my trajectory and landed a good 40 yards from the stump. I managed to lose the running chainsaw when the tree let loose, and I don't know how long it ran before running out of gas. So displaced, I found myself when I awoke.

Ignoring the dwarf, who I was sure was a hallucination, I started at my toes and began moving individual body parts. All seemed to move, most hurt, so my spine was probably intact. My left leg was twisted at an unusual angle and was surely broken. It was, in fact, a compound fracture. I managed to lift my head high enough to see the jagged white femur protruding from the tear in my blood-soaked Levi's. My arms functioned pain free, and I began exploring the damage with my hands. I hesitated to move my torso until I was absolutely certain my back was not injured. I am not a doctor but some injuries are easy to diagnose—a protruding bone for example. The pain in my chest suggested broken ribs and a punctured lung, perhaps bruised and split spleen and liver. I considered the possibility of my death.

I tried to move, to turn over and try to rise. The dwarf was on me like a slap. No hallucination this. He held me down, a gentle hand on my forehead, while he poured a bitter fluid into my mouth from an old army canteen. My last conscious emotion was fear. I had dreams.

In my dreams, I heard my truck engine growling, moving in first gear. I heard myself scream, eyes open in sightless pain. I felt my body twisted in agony. Later I knew comfort. In my dreams, I heard my chainsaw and the crack of a whip. Felt the surprise of flight, heard the murmur of death.

I don't usually remember dreams, nor do I dream in color, but these dreams have stayed in me through the years, crimson and green memories of my time in flight, my time with the dwarf.

I awoke at sundown, groggy from what I knew was a drug-induced sleep. My first reaction was a renewal of the fear I felt when the dwarf poured the drug in my mouth. The fear subsided when I realized the little man was gone. I turned my head to see if he was still watching. Instead, I found myself staring at a blue tarp forming a lean-to above me. It looked like the one I carry in my truck, but then there are a million blue tarps. I remembered my injuries, but not from the pain. I inched my hands down my body. There was a corset around my rib cage. It felt substantial but not elastic. I jerked involuntarily when I thought of the jagged femur edge. My hand crept to my damaged thigh. I found another binding and a straightened leg. Could the midget have done this? I thought there must be paramedics nearby, waiting to helicopter me out of my predicament, but I could neither see nor hear anyone.

Something was wearing off. My wounds began to throb. The pain rose in waves. I thought of Ravel's Bolero. Where were the dwarf and his canteen? Then he was next to me, calm, a smile on his oversized face. I reached for the canteen, and he let me take it.

New dreams. Dreams of work, of cutting wood, stacking wood, burning wood. I dreamt of falling trees and falling water, of broken limbs and broken bones. I was in my own body, inspecting my lungs, my liver and spleen. Covered in blood, I dove in my heart at the opening of my aortic valve. I was swallowed in a red tornado. Sucked in, sluiced down a blue tube to a dead end at a jagged white-yellow ridge, squirted out on a denim sponge.

I awoke under a hot sun, exhausted, hungry, and wondering why no help had come. The tarp was gone. I thought of my friend, and he came. This time he gave me cool water. He didn't allow me to drink all I wanted.

It occurred to me to talk. "Who are you?" My voice was weak, my pain great. "Thank you for the water. Did you do this for me? Can you help me get home?" Saying these few things exhausted me. The dwarf moved close, put his large hand on my forehead, feeling for fever? It must be. He took my pulse. Then he stood, large head looking ready to roll off his small body, short arms crossed, dwarf face pursed in thought. Penguinlike, he moved out of my sight. I was afraid to be alone.

I wanted to move, but I found that I was tied to the logs that lay on each side of me. I tried to yell, but then I heard my truck start, rev, move in first gear. Then silence, a slamming door, quick footsteps in the brush. More sounds of cracking limbs and hurried steps. I was more curious than fearful. I wanted to see my friend, to ask him what he was doing. I could only stare at the limitless sky.

The plume started slowly, a white wisp rising in the windless forest. Soon it was thick, and roiled skyward with the intensity of flowing lava. I would be found soon. During a blink, an eye squeeze to clear my tears, my savior reappeared, sweaty, breathing hard. He cut my bonds and removed the chest and leg wraps. I yelped in pain. He dragged away the logs and that was the last I saw him.

The plane appeared in fifteen minutes, twenty-six seconds. I know because I counted. The police and paramedics arrived soon thereafter. Then my wife. Words would not come. Tears came, running from my cheeks to the young ferns below. I cried myself to sleep. No dreams.

It was three months before I could get back to where it happened. Even then my wife insisted on accompanying me. In those three months I told my story to only a handful of people, none of whom believed me. The doctors explained my leg wound: A sharp limb pierced my quadriceps and fractured my femur. The x-ray showed a clean fracture, perfectly aligned. No one questioned the lack of debris in the wound. No need to explain the broken ribs and punctured lung. I was struck like a baseball. Something had to give.

My story didn't agree with the way my truck was found, bed full with sixteen-inch lengths of firewood, some elm, perhaps a tree's worth, the rest rock maple and beech, both excellent woods. Nor would anyone believe that it wasn't me that started the signal fire. They thought I was most likely unconscious from Saturday morning to early Monday when I awoke and somehow managed to drag myself around the forest floor gathering an estimated half-ton of firewood and brush in such a combination of dry and damp so as to provide an absolutely monolithic column of white smoke a quarter mile high. My small friend? Merely the fevered dreams of an injured man, lucky to be alive.

I showed my wife where to park. My injured leg still hurt to operate the stiff clutch. I got out of the truck and began searching for the trigger stump. The late August ferns were high, but the group of dead elms told me I was close. I could not find it and was getting frustrated until I realized I had to look up, look for two scarred trees close together. They were obvious. I could see where the elm had plowed between them, stripping their branches, forcing them to a cocked attitude. I grew gooseflesh in the August heat. From them it was easy to locate the stump, the place I stood, my launching pad. I knew the elm would be gone.

My wife waited patiently while I studied the area. My flight direction was easy to determine. I walked slowly, studying the trees. Several showed signs of recent broken limbs. One branch, twenty feet high, flew a small denim flag, ragged from the wind.

I tried hard to find where I landed or where the dwarf tended to my wounds, gave me water, saved my life. There was no sign, no evidence. I stood in the afternoon forest, a feeling of loss growing within me. I sensed he was near, but I could not see him. Was it all a dream? I touched my leg, felt the scar, remembered the canteen. I did not care who thought what, who believed and who didn't. I was here and he was here, and I am alive today because of him.

We drove home in silence, my wife angry at my mood, me, angry at my loss. That night I slept poorly. I had dreams.

In my dreams I floated amid a green kingdom, full of men of small stature. The kingdom existed in the boughs of leafy trees. I dreamt of medicinal ointments, healing balms, oils of succor. My body floated on chlorophyll foam, safe from jagged discomforts. I was dressed in tailored bark clothing, neat, smooth fitting. I felt good, and I felt I knew what only the dead know, but I did not know what it was. I dreamt of a lost forest, lush with strange vegetation, silent but for a lone saw, whining against a smoke-white dead trunk, the trunk reaching past sight into an unknown sky.

Petoskey Bear River Mother ©2023 Moon Seagren

Newsprint

Art Curtis

"Brinley Beagle, 9, of Alba, reacts after a water balloon breaks
above his head,
drenching him in cold water.
"It felt nice 'cause it's hotter than heck out here," Beagle said.
(Caption, front page, *Antrim County News*, 8/3/2017)

I see this as I crumble
news of the past
into fire starter.

I work my way backwards
now, in late November,
already back to August.

Not that it's been that cold
but I have felt the need for comfort
felt the need for warmth

need the heat of desire
the flames of passion
to warm myself to purpose.

There's irony as I twist
Beagle's words and image
into fodder for my match

that these balls of newsprint
overlaid with dried bark and cedar,
split maple and oak are essential

for the same sense of heat
Beagle escaped temporarily
in the burst of a water balloon.

Even last August, I was cold.

Black Dog

Monique Bova

She flushed three deer the other day
Disappearing like a glossy black
Spearpoint
Into the swamp
The snapping of her body
Open and closed
So different than her usual happy meander
We wondered at her sudden
Primal determination
Even as we worried that the wolf inside
Would run her completely out of our influence

Black dog
Our eyes locked on her exit
Even as the swamp exploded behind us
Frost brittled cedar giving way
To the mad edge of panic
Brown blurs
So often viewed as distant triangles
Bent in gentle graze
But now
Driven from their beds
White flags
Not of surrender
But their own
Primal determination
To escape, to escape

And us in their barreling path
Vulnerable as prey

Black dog
With the mindful mindlessness
Of ancient instinct
Casting 'round
Behind
Fetching the herd
Which careened by
Close enough to make me step back
In the wind they made
And at their heels
Black dog
Ears meeting at the top
Of each joyful bound
Then down again
With a smack of released momentum
On either side
Of her flapping
Squint-eyed
Grin

Harvest Moon ©2023 Karen Walker

An Old Man's Treasure

Betsy Hayhow Hemming

With some trepidation, I entered the little cabin for the first time. After so many years of fearing the old man's wrath, it almost seemed an act of courage to walk through the doorway.

I shuddered from the damp chill, surprising on an unseasonably spring-like March afternoon. It was actually warmer outside than in. Darkness and dust wrapped us in a quiet cloak. It quickly became apparent that the old man's possessions remained untouched, even though Mr. Standish had died nearly a year ago. Our family bought the cabin from his nephews, his only living relatives.

The questions danced around my head like gnats. How could his family just leave everything? What was he really like? Most importantly, why had he hated little children so much?

I knew a bit about this man, this old curmudgeon who lived alone here for so many years. His cabin was one of about twenty on a small northern Michigan lake. My grandparents also owned a cabin on the lake, and I spent many a summer's day blissfully consuming all the joys of the lake and surrounding woods. My grandparents passed away years ago, leaving their cabin to their beloved children and grandchildren. My parents—now grandparents themselves—finally decided that a nearby cabin of our own would offer more quality lake time to our growing family. When they learned that Mr. Standish's cabin was on the market, they quickly made an offer, and much to our delight, they became the new owners.

In the living area, years-old television listings scattered on the coffee table clearly served as a restroom stop for a passing mouse. A war novel lay open on a footstool. I could imagine a fire crackling in the big stone fireplace, even on a balmy March day, a tired man taking a break from his outside chores and reading a chapter or two from his novel.

A wall of faded curtains separated the bedroom from the living area. Taped scraps of paper filled with Detroit Tigers baseball scores covered one wall. A dusty radio propped on a windowsill offered an image of the old fellow lying in bed on a hot summer night, with barely a hint of a lake breeze, listening to the announcer call the game. How solitary his life must have been, as he jotted down the scores and taped them to the wall, the adult me mused.

But the child me had a decidedly different view, of an old tyrant who hated kids with a passion. We all knew the rules back then: "Stay away from Mr. Standish's cabin!" parents and grandparents admonished. Did we? Of course not, and for a perfectly valid reason: Old Mr. Standish's tree-covered valley behind his cabin served as an absolute haven for the kids who enjoyed summers on the lake. We spent hours imagining this land as a battlefield, for closely fought wars and other dramatic endeavors. The law of attraction lured us there again and again. What did it hurt him if we did a little war re-enactment on his precious property?

Our military excursions often involved Mr. Standish himself. He would stalk out of his cabin waving a broom or a shovel, loudly yelling, "Git off my property!" We would flee the valley as if the enemy was were tight on our heels. Regrouping at the beach, our sweaty crew of soldiers would offer exaggerated views of the conflict:

"He is so mean; I thought he was going to whack you with that shovel!"

"He can't catch me; he's too old; he's gonna die soon."

"No way! He's gonna live forever 'cause he's cursed."

"Yeah! He's cursed 'cause he killed his true love!"

Yes, many tall tales resulted from our debriefs. My favorite was that Mr. Standish had been a miser, hiding away a fortune somewhere in the cabin or on the grounds, which included a two-story shed and an old garage. My young self imagined a fellow who had loved and lost many decades ago. Overcome with grief, he hid his treasure where no one would ever find it.

All these years later, I still believed that hidden treasure was what provoked Mr. Standish's loathing of our crew of child soldiers so long ago. He just didn't want any of us finding the mother lode. It made perfect sense to me. Ever-idealistic, I decided to keep an eye out for nooks and crannies that might offer a perfect hiding place for a fortune.

We began the process of cleaning and moving into the cabin. We took armfuls of clothing out of dresser drawers and packed them up for the Salvation Army. A new television replaced the little black and white set that had been there for so many years, and we took down the baseball scores and threw them away.

One day, while we were working to clean a very decrepit kitchen, my father found a firecracker hidden above the doorway. But before my active imagination could take over, Dad discounted the find. "The old geezer hated dogs more than he did kids," he said. "I'm told he kept firecrackers around to scare them off."

I sighed and went back to washing the walls.

We did keep a few mementos. We found several old kerosene lamps and stored them out on the back porch in case of a power outage. We would make great use of them in the years ahead. The big gas stove in the kitchen made fine scrambled eggs on weekend mornings, even though the oven never worked. Perhaps the most treasured possession of all was the long wooden table on the front porch, where many enjoyable dinners found us solving the great mysteries of life, accompanied by candles, wine, and the sound of crickets and frogs out by the lake.

The war novel that had been tossed on the footstool actually found a home on the bookshelf, and I confess I opened it up one rainy afternoon some years later while my children were napping. It was gory, and I gave it up after a few chapters, chuckling. Of course Mr. Standish would have appreciated a good book on war.

As my kids grew older, they enjoyed the same games and drama that I remembered from childhood, much like the adage that old jokes hang in the air of elementary classrooms year after year. The kids initiated their own wars in the valley, but the only booming voice they heard was that of their grandfather, informing them it was time to pick up sticks, clean the decks, or some other horror. They, too, searched for treasure, having heard my stories of the past, but not with the same conviction. I still kept my eye out for possible hiding places when the kids weren't watching.

One summer, several years after we had purchased the cabin, Dad and I decided to transform the second floor of the old shed into a fort for the grandkids. The first floor had long served as Dad's tool room, and the upper floor was left to accumulate spider webs and pine cone debris from squirrels' breakfasts. Our first step was to undertake a robust cleaning, as dreary as that sounded.

Dad carted his nifty toolbox up the musty stairway, and I followed with the shop vac. We spent hours cleaning and repairing the funny old shed, laughing at the fact that we were spending one of northern Michigan's impeccable summer days in such a hot, dusty hideaway. Sweating profusely, we simultaneously eyed the second-story window, which had been nailed shut for as long as we had owned the property. We figured a little fresh air would help the cause, and we started pulling out nails.

Dad abruptly stopped work. "Look here," he said. "I found something." He pointed to a small cupboard above the window, which we had never seen before. It looked oddly out of place and was locked with a small padlock. I caught my breath. What possible reason could there be for a small, locked cupboard on the second level of a dirty old shed?

While my mind went wild with ideas, Dad calmly sawed off the lock and opened the cupboard door. He peered inside and shook his head. I trembled with excitement. "I just knew he had treasure hidden here," I exclaimed.

Smiling at my abrupt return to childhood, he pulled out a set of dusty old papers and quickly scanned them. "Owner's manual for the lake pump," he solemnly reported. My shoulders slumped as he returned for another look inside.

This time, he pulled out a long, slender bundle, wrapped in a grimy gray cloth. I uttered a shriek and twirled around like my twelve-year-old dancing daughter. "Open it, open it!" I commanded.

Dad shook his head, smiling at my outburst. He slowly unwrapped the cloth and took a long look. He snorted and began to chortle.

"What is it?" I cried out impatiently. I knew it had to be money, jewelry, or both. I stopped twirling and leaned toward him, desperate to get a look.

"Here's your hidden treasure, my dear," Dad said, still chuckling. He reached out and handed me the three firecrackers that had been carefully stored under lock and key for so many years, the perfect gift from a frustrated and lonely old man.

Evening Solitude ©2023 Karen Walker

In Between Days

Thomas Ford Conlan

When the cool of autumn comes round,
wild sunflowers glow and the sweet corn
cries to be plucked,
summer birds have gone south
yet I still top off the feeder.

Salmon run out in the Big Lake,
taste like sweet marmalade on the grill,
but I ponder the sweet corn,
put on a jacket against the north breeze,
and miss another fleeting chance to fish.

Glorious September, when the tourists
return south with the birds,
and children answer calling school bells.
Quiet anticipation floats in the gentle air
and the first maple leaves show a tinge of yellow.

I should be fishing, with a precious few days left in the season.
Choices must be made, priorities settled. But a fullness envelopes me.
I will pass the Zen morning, wait while the sun burns off the dew,
and later, put up the sweet corn, savoring fresh morsels,
frozen to last through the coming cold.

September

Katy Klimczuk

The beginning
and end

Warm days
Cool nights

Beckoning me
inward

Resistance

I don't want to go
into the abyss

The flowers and water
Alive with color

Still

Bees buzz
Sunflowers stretch

And yet

The leaves blush

Gold, bronze, and burgundy

The sun lowers its crown of rays

Lean in
cozy up

"Until next year," says the marmalade moon

Pileated Woodpecker ©2023 Greg Young

Red Squirrel ©2023 Greg Young

Autumn Comes/Winter Calls

Gary Schils

1.
On Lost Lake Li Po paddles
his canoe, a small keg of beer, a tent
a blanket and a bag of mixed nuts his only cargo.
He looks at the palm of his hand
and sees the naked body of his mistress dancing,
swirling lightly as if on a music box.

Solitude and time wake him from this dream.
The music stops.
Even the whippoorwills fall silent.
A blister blossoms on the palm of his left hand
but not from pirouettes.

As the drifter drifts,
memories swirl like paddle strokes
dissipating into dark waters.
The good days course through his mind
as the river beneath his canoe.

2.
Seeking ground to make camp Li Po wonders,
*"Have I wasted my life
fishing rivers and streams for trout?"*
His bank account tells him so.
Careful not to scratch the bottom
of his craft on the gravel shore,

he gently banks his canoe.
Before setting camp, he stands
and scans the river for rising trout.
No one from city-bank will deposit
this investment but Li Po does not give a damn.

3.
Years pass.
Li Po's hair is white as a cloud.
His canoe, upside down, gathers dust.
He lies by a creek, a stone for a pillow,
the autumn leaves above brighter than June flowers.

His eight decades are like a field of ferns
leaning on one another for support against the wind.
A brown thrasher, talking in tongues,
tells his kind, *"It's time to go! It's time to go!"*

As the creek converses with the stones
Li Po hears voices of lovers past.
He used to bound from rock to rock
like a mink. Youth was his animal.

Now his mind is his animal.
As he reads, his head resting on a rock,
he imagines a flock of Sandhill Cranes
soaring beyond the sky as the pages
in his book turn into wings.

His body is as still as the Miocene
crane fossil found in Nebraska,
ten million years old, but his mind . . .
his mind is a bird that never rests.

The Good Wife

for Sylvia

Gary Schils

Here's to wild trout and leak-less waders,
Here's to tight lines and drag free floats,
Here's to my good wife who waits for me
And calls my name from the river's edge.

Here's to mayfly hatches and bright waters,
Here's to clear skies and mild winds,
Here's to my good wife who waits for me,
Her body scented with peppermint oil.

Here's to clean sheets and covers rolled down,
Here's to my wife in her pretty summer dress,
She calls my name from sweet, minted lips,
She calls my name from the river's edge.

Here's to brook trout and red spots in blue halos,
Here's to articulated mazes of vermiculation.
She will smile when she sees my creel full of trout.
She will smile when a half a dozen are in the sink.

Here's to my wife who tugs on my boots
And wipes down my fly rod with a damp cloth.
Faithfully she melts butter in the frying pan,
Garlic, onions and salted pink flesh.

Here's to clean sheets and peppermint skin,
Here's to wild trout and clear swift rivers,
Rivers that run strong as my love for my wife
When she calls my name from the river's edge.

A Fly Angler's Musings

Paul Maxbauer

I stand in the river and wait for the Giant
Michigan Mayflies to appear, wait for
trout to rise. Wait, watch, and listen.
Very warm and muggy, perspiration
beads on my forehead from my walk
through the woods. Mosquitoes buzz,
pester my ears and neck. In the low light
I struggle to thread the tippet through the
hook eye before cinching the knot.

I glance upstream then down, listen for
the sound of fish feeding. Small
insects skitter near the river's surface.
Two robins call from the tall cedars.
I light a cigar to pass the time, and
ward off mosquitoes.

The sky is a dark blue vault with
a growing array of bright stars. On the
horizon bands of pale light above the
treetops glow yellow, orange, and pink.
Along the banks dark shadows cast by the
trees give way to a silvery flow in the
middle of the river, while a half-moon
ascends.

A deer emerges from a meadow across
the river, lowers its nose to the water
and drinks, then moves back in the shadows.
A muskrat swims along the far bank, and
disappears in the tall grass. A two-foot snake
swims downstream directly at me, circles
around my legs as if I were a tree stump,
then continues down river.

Nature's comings and goings, and timing the
big mayfly hatch, remain a mystery, like family
and friends who parade through episodes of
our lives, important for a time, then present
only in memories.

I check my watch. It is getting late, well past
the time for the hatch to start. As I walk back
to the car, my flashlight finds the trail, now a
narrow, lighted tunnel through the dark woods.
When I arrive home near mid-night, the outdoor
light is on. There to greet me at the back door is
a Giant Michigan Mayfly, clinging to the screen.

Spring Fever

Paul Maxbauer

I woke this morning to fresh snow,
a lovely winter scene outside the
window. Large flakes filled the sky,
slanted downward, coated tree branches
and the cone shaped cedars on the edge
of a neighbor's yard.

A thick blanket of snow covered the
sidewalks and streets, the gray, opaque
ice newly hidden. New snow lay on
the grimy piles heaped-up by plows,
and looked very much like a January
landscape, all dressed in white.

But the calendar shows mid-March,
and I am weary of the snow and ice,
so I go back to bed, close my eyes,
hope to dream of a different scene,
of blue sky and sunshine, early shoots
of green grass, flowers, trees in bloom,
robins and mourning doves on newly
built nests.

I floated a river, paddled slowly,
a sun dappled day, swallows worked
the sky, the riverbanks were alive in
vibrant greens, clumps of white dogwood,

and goldenrod. The river ran low
and clear, free of winter's icy grip.
That is where dreams take me.

Winter on the Jordan River ©2023 Doug Pfaff

The Bones of My Heart

Melissa Seitz

After several hours of light snow whipping itself around by erratic easterly winds, I venture out onto the frozen lake to figure out a plan. Higgins Lake, smooth and slippery, seems like an ice rink in late January. I am not a skater. In a small area somehow missed by snowfall, I stare at the sand and rocks below me. I feel as if I am on top of a giant aquarium. Nothing moves below me. The ice appears to be strong enough to support my weight. If I fall through, I remind myself that I will only be up to my shoulders. I convince myself that my sturdy hockey-mom legs should be able to get me out of any trouble I might find myself in. It is time for me to create the first heart of the year on the lake.

I begin my work by walking in a giant heart-shaped pattern after I determine a few things. The first heart is always the most difficult one to design. Where should I place it? I consider the angle of the sun in the morning, the likely movement of the ice as it continues to settle, and my vantage point from shore. What will I see from the beach? The house? Once I map out the initial heart, I walk over it a few times to create a solid outline. This year's first heart seems delicate, because I do not have much snow to work with to create a strong base. I hope for the best. Where I place the bones of my first heart of winter is incredibly important to me.

The days pass by, and the temperatures continue to drop. The ice covers more and more of the lake. I begin to journey out farther to make more hearts, especially if we receive more snowfall. Dogs, deer, fox, coyotes, or people will eventually walk across my hearts. My family has strict orders to avoid stepping into a heart. Snowmobilers and cross-country skiers always manage to cut through my hearts and do the most damage.

I once read a quote by Thich Nhat Hanh that said, "The sun is our heart outside of the body." A good friend had recently suggested I read his work. That saying spoke to me. I had been shooting photos of the sunrise for many years, and I had started making large hearts out on the frozen lake in front of our house somewhere along the line. My hearts were for the sunrise and for Nicole. Our daughter died four days after she was born thirty-five years ago. The grief, firmly etched into my own heart, needed a way to reveal itself especially during the month of February when she had been born and then died.

During sunrise, grief flares up like the sharpest of sunbeams. On gray days, sorrow still hides behind the clouds, only muted, as if someone promised me something but forgot to follow through on it. On beautiful days, the ones where it seems as if the sun will burn a hole straight through my heart, I feel her presence in hope, longing, loss, love, sadness, sorrow, anger, and yet, I always return to hope. I am still alive. Hearts remind me of that. So does sunrise.

If not for my husband, son, and several close friends who have walked this long grief journey with me, I do not know where I would be. It is true that I can only create my hearts on the lake during the months of January, February, March, and into April, but I have hearts everywhere in my house. Glass hearts, wooden hearts, painted hearts, clothing with hearts, earrings, pins, and necklaces with hearts are inside, and outside, I have windchimes with hearts. I think Nicole would approve.

Recently, we had a big snowstorm, the kind the weather people talk about for days and days, and my hearts went missing. Once I made it through the drifts in our yard, I climbed down through a narrow ridge of snow about 8–9 inches deep that had built up along the shoreline. I walked out a few more feet and stepped through several inches of snow into about 3 inches of slush. The lake can be surprising that way. It was wet, sloppy, watery, and cold. I created a small heart—only about 6 feet by 6 feet. My hearts are never precise.

When the latest snow begins to melt, I will search for my old hearts. If we get another snow storm, I will need to create a new heart. The older hearts might eventually appear. Only time will tell. Eventually, most of the snow will melt and the ice will reveal the outlines of my hearts—the bones. Sometimes, my hearts end up being on top of each other or they overlap. As spring nears, the larger body of ice starts to diminish, and my hearts break into pieces and melt. I will, of course, wait for sunrise. I have never been disappointed with the beauty nature provides me so early in the morning.

I am on year six of not missing a sunrise photo no matter where I have been. Sunrise time is when I can talk to the sky, God, Nicole, the birds, the lake, the mountains in Colorado, Route 66 in Oklahoma, the Arches in Utah, on a boat in the Sea of Cortez, the top of Brockway Mountain in Michigan's Upper Peninsula, or Marquette, Michigan, as a freighter chugs by, or think about anything I want—uninterrupted. No one will bother me. Well, that is not true. Occasionally, I have had people show up for sunrise, and that is fine. Those were special occasions. Other moments where I have been awestruck and filled with love at the same time were when an eagle swooped down for a fish and surprised me, or those mornings when loons send out warning tremolos that cause me to search the sky for danger as I stand along the shore. During winter one year, when the lake was frozen over, a fox ran in front of me, gave me a look as if I was trespassing, and then ran faster to get away from me. I moved just enough to shoot some photos. I talked about that fox for a few years to anyone who would listen. As a matter of fact, I still talk about that fox, and I have seen other foxes on the ice since then. None have stopped to give me a look like that one did.

I start the day, too, with whatever song pops into my head—there sure are a lot of Beatles songs locked into my memory files—and then I listen to the sounds around me. In winter, sometimes the ice groans or roars as if it cannot quite make up its mind. Those hearts I create eventually disappear into the water as if they never existed. This is like people, I suppose. When our loved ones die, all we have left are the memories of them and lots of photographs if we are lucky. One thing we can do is go outside every morning at sunrise and sing a song about them if it helps. The song does not have to make sense. As a matter of fact, many, many months after Nicole died, I started singing one day in the kitchen when my late mother was at our house. My mother stopped what she was doing and looked at me. She said, "I think you will be alright." I had not sung anything for a such a long time that my mother had become extremely concerned about me. I looked at her, and I told her that I was not sure. I continued singing my made-up song about baking cookies.

I understand now that grief is a heartbreak song. The lyrics and the song itself change all the time. When I watch the sunrise in the morning, it gives me hope for all kinds of reasons. I will look forward to spring again this year and the way that the lake reveals itself to us again. In April, I will search out on the ice for pieces of my hearts. As east winds push the ice up against our shore, I will watch the eventual crumbling. Ducks will wait impatiently to come into our yard, and loons will start arriving out by the drop-off and sing the songs of spring. One morning, the ice will be completely gone, and the lake will be free of winter's cradle. I will sit on the shore and watch the sunrise. I will place my hands down into the sand on our beach and trace the outline of a heart. The sand will be cold and most likely wet, but it will feel good to start something new once again. I will feel it in my bones.

Sunrise Sun Pillar ©2023 Melissa Seitz

Stepping Out

Deda Kavanagh

settling
to absorb pine limbs
shrouding nightshade

bending
to tend the dead
leaves in the gazing globe

dodging winter
dry hibiscus
in the face vase

gravestone
two women keening
crows hang gliding

Drummond Island
ruffed grouse wings beat
the doldrums

last oak leaf
stem stuck
in blue ice

   one trout upstream
one down
  stars their cargo

No Place Like Home

Bridget Klaasen

We are Parkers, not Travelers, and my grandparents on the Parker side, although they often spoke of how much they would like to cross the Mackinac Bridge, rarely made it past Grayling, where they visited Cousin Rita who lived in a one-bedroom house in town where she could walk everywhere she needed to go. Someone made a railing out of iron pipe for her to hold onto to get down the step so maybe she didn't walk well but she walked every day. She always walked to Ben Franklin. She liked the candy counter and the way the floor creaked. She liked the doll-sized bottles of perfume and the handkerchiefs. She didn't use hankies, but she liked pansy prints and was tempted, always, to slip one into her pocket but she never did. Cousin Rita loved seafoam candy. She said it made her mouth giggle. Grandma said Rita was cute when she giggled, and the way she said it made Rita sound like a windup toy.

Grandma made date pinwheel cookies to take when they went to visit Rita, and she left money in Rita's change purse for the candy. "Don't spend it all at once," Grandma warned, "or you could laugh your pants right off!" and this, of course, made Rita giggle even more. Rita was what you would call simple. She had a very small head.

"Small headed people live to be a hundred," my grandma on my mother's side said. Grandma Hirsch was a believer in phrenology, a so-called science that enabled her to decree newcomers "sneaky" at first glance.

"Small heads, small minds," my mother said, not because she, too, was a believer but because she always had to have the last word.

I don't know who inherited Cousin Rita when Grandma and Grandpa died. Probably Aunt Edie. She was the most reliable. When her daughter turned school age, Aunt Edie got a job in a factory that made pickles. Her job was to pack them in jars. She said she would work until she saved up enough for new drapes.

She stayed at that job thirty-five years.

"Pretty expensive curtains," my mother said.

Edie had the kind of handwriting that came from beautiful hands, not hard-working hands. She could do anything with her hands. She could decorate cakes, making icing flowers with the smallest of tips, she could embroider without a transfer pattern, she could make lace and trimmed all her daughter's socks with it, she could knit and crochet and even went so far as to make a needlepoint portrait of President Kennedy after he was shot. It looked like him, too—his eyes could undress you from any point in the room.

She had talent, but she also had luck. "Some people are just plain, lucky," my mother said, discounting that while she spent her evenings drinking Southern Comfort, neat, out of a water glass, Edie was using her perfect penmanship to fill out contest entry forms. Edie did this every night, regular as saying her prayers. She won. She won a sewing machine and a set of encyclopedias and a canister vacuum and a top loading washer and then she won the grand prize:

a trip to Europe courtesy of Kraft mayonnaise.

That one really pissed my mother off. "What do those people do with all the mayonnaise they buy," she demanded to know. "They can't possibly be eating it all?"

She had a point. Aunt Edie did have the odds stacked in her favor. She steamed the labels off a lot of jars to win, and truth be told, the grand prize wasn't the one she wanted. She really wanted the Speed Queen oven, but her husband, who had never been farther from home than deer camp, patted her on the ass for the first time in twenty years, and said, "C'mon, baby, we got front row seats on a TWA jet!"

They were gone seven days and when asked where they went, Aunt Edie started with Detroit: "Detroit, Paris, Brussels, Rome, and Zurich," she said, counting cities off on her fingers like birthday cards to drop in the mail.

When they returned, we went to Grandma and Grandpa's for Sunday dinner, like we did every Sunday because Grandma thought one meal a week that her children didn't have to plan or pay for was a blessing. She always served candied apple slices in a cut glass dish, which wasn't much of a treat for my mother, but she enjoyed the roast chicken. Most nights we had cereal or pancakes for dinner because Mom had to pay a payment on a car my dad couldn't afford. "Can't wait," she told him, as he backed the Thunderbird out of the too-small garage, "to wash dishes for eight people while your dad stretches out in his Barcalounger and lights a cigar."

We expected to hear about Aunt Edie's trip, but she didn't have much to say. When pressed, she said she didn't care for the food and Uncle Baldy, who had a huge head that refused to grow hair, said the chairs weren't very comfortable, and they both said they had to wait in a lot of lines, lines for everything, and it was very crowded. Then Aunt Edie gave me a souvenir. It was a medallion the size of a dime, probably not worth more than that, with the pope's face on it, making it worth a million times that. She said she waited in line all afternoon to have it blessed by the pope, so a zillion times more valuable than a dime, and she said to my mother, "That is what you Catlicks do, right?" and the whole table stared at my mother and my mother said, "Yes. That, and perform exorcisms. Without anesthesia."

My grandma asked if she could pass anyone anything. "More chicken, there is still a wing and a thigh?" she asked.

Aunt Edie said no thank you, she had enough, and she meant enough chicken, enough of my mother, and enough travel. She wanted to stay home and never go anywhere again, to set her self-cleaning oven to clean, her dishwasher to heated dry, wrap her hair in a scarf, and wake up before the alarm sounded. She had enough travel to last a lifetime.

How was she to know Grandma and Grandpa were planning a trip?

Grandma held firm that she wanted to ride across the Mighty Mac, and Grandpa confessed he always wanted to see the Soo locks. They thought they should offer someone else a chance to see it, too, and they settled on Baldy and Edie because they had experience. They set out, Grandpa and Baldy in the front seat and Grandma and Edie in the back, each working on a different afghan. Edie could make cable patterns without looking down, and on the way home they couldn't decide which was the best attraction, the bridge or the locks, both of which were more impressive than any painted ceiling Edie had seen. She said that over and over. They were giddy with joy and bought gifts for everyone: a jackknife for my dad and a spoonrest for my mom and a pencil case for me and the best of all, a ViewMaster that came with packaged slides of other attractions. Edie said the slide of the tulip festival in Holland, Michigan was 100x better than Holland—Holland and the ones of the bridge and the Locks looked exactly the same as being there.

"Can you imagine that?" they asked, and when they pulled into the driveway, Grandma said, "Ahh, home sweet home," and that was the last trip she ever took.

20th Annual Crooked Tree Arts Center Juried Young Writers Exposition

Walloon Writers Review is delighted to share the winners of the 2022 20th Annual Crooked Tree Arts Center Juried Young Writers Exposition. This event is a collaboration between Crooked Tree Arts Center, Petoskey News-Review, the Bob Schultze Fund for Creative Writing at the Petoskey-Harbor Springs Area Community Foundation, Little Traverse Literary Guild, McLean & Eakin Booksellers of Petoskey, and Walloon Writers Review.

Poetry/1ˢᵗ Place *Reese Hoffman*

5ᵗʰ grade Saint Francis Xavier

On the Farm

On the farm where the long grass grows,
And the gentle wind blows,
And the birds fly through the trees,
The deer run across the fields
and everything here is free.

On the farm with the animal sounds,
and the kittens playing all around.
I feel such a relaxing charm
In my mother's home cooked meals

While the horses rest in the barn
On the farm you hear the roosters call,
And my siblings and I throw around the ball,
There's not a reason to frown,
not a happier place appeals,
 Playing until the sun goes down.

G.O.A.T. Squad

BAM! BOOM! The potato guns were firing everywhere. The tomato grenades were exploding all around them. The G.O.A.T. Squad was covered, and they had nowhere to go.

Yesterday:

It was a hot Colorado day on their farm. It was also lunchtime for the G.O.A.T. Squad. The G.O.A.T. Squad is an elite group of goats that go on secret missions. One morning when they walked into the barn to get their grain, they realized that someone took it. They were shocked. They couldn't believe that someone took the most elite group of goats' food. They all agreed that night that they would search the farm to find the perpetrator.

That night, the G.O.A.T. Squad put on all of their night vision equipment and headed out. It was very quiet, and they had to be careful that they didn't make any noise. They checked the pig's barn first. After asking some questions they decided that the pigs were too lazy to steal the food, and they would've made such a racket that all of the farm animals would think that a twister was going through. Interrogating the pigs had taken so much time that they could only go to one more animal barn. They discussed it and decided that they would go to the big animal barn. They had to split up so that they could question more animals at once. Again, they hit a dead end. That could only mean that the chickens took their grain. The chickens had a bad reputation so they would interrogate them in the morning when they could wear all of their gear.

The next morning, they checked to make sure that their gear was ready in case the chickens tried to attack. They made sure their potato guns and tomato grenades were in working order. Then BAM, they kicked down the barn door. They caught the chickens red handed. Some of them were even eating the grain. ATTACK! The G.O.A.T. Squad charged. The chickens charged. The goats were clearly outnumbered and outgunned. BAM! BOOM! POW! The goats took cover behind some haystacks. BAM! BOOM! The potato guns were firing everywhere. Tomatoes were exploding everywhere. The G.O.A.T. Squad was covered, and they had nowhere to go. They had some things though that the chickens would never have, the ability to eat anything. After taking a deep breath, they charged towards the chickens eating all of the tomatoes and potatoes. It took the chickens by surprise. The chickens ran away, but the G.O.A.T. Squad caught up and put them in wingcuffs. Then the goats sent them away to bird jail.

The next day the goats were interrogating the chickens in their cell when they discovered an awful truth…the chickens were part of a secret mafia called the E.G.G., which stands for Evil Grain Grabbers. After pushing on the chickens, they learned that the E.G.G. headquarters is under the Empire State Building in New Pork. The headquarters could only be opened by a special key card at room 111. They tried to tempt the chickens to get a key card and it worked. Once they were finished, they wrapped things up and headed back to the farm. Now they had to get some rest because it was going to be a long trip to New Pork.

The next day, they got themselves ready and boarded an airplane destined for New Pork. During the flight they called President Woodchuck Wilson because they needed a pumpkin launcher tank in case a fight broke out between the G.O.A.T. Squad and the E.G.G., and they needed some backup.

When they landed in New Pork, they were greeted by the U.S. Army Ants at the airport. After that they got into a helicopter and headed to the secret base where they would be staying until the E.G.G. were defeated.

The next day, they received the tank and were ready for battle. When they left, they got an escort by the police to the Empire State Building. Once they got there the Army Ants stayed with the tank outside and the goats went up to room 111 and put the card in. CREAK. The door slowly swung open. There were already some chickens there. CRACK! The goats knocked out the chickens but not before the chickens sounded the alarm. CLUCK, CLUCK! The G.O.A.T Squad ran outside hoping that the chickens would follow them. When the chickens ran out it sent a chill down the goat's spine. There were at least 100 chickens. Pumpkins were flying everywhere. The Army Ants and goats were shooting potatoes and throwing tomato grenades everywhere. Some of the chickens were in such a hurry to get the goats that some of them forgot their weapons. In no time, the Army Ants and G.O.A.T. Squad surrounded the E.G.G. and they were arrested. They were all sent to bird jail. Now people could eat their grain without worrying that the E.G.G. would take it.

Later that week, President Woodchuck Wilson awarded them the medal of honor for their bravery.

The End

Whispers Behind Me

I hear something soft and quiet.
A whisper.
I turn around to see
Kids whispering and looking at me.
I feel self-conscious,
So I turn my head and look away.
Are they whispering about me?
What I look like, how I feel?
I try to push it away
But it comes back every single day.
How do I get rid of it?
Now I'm back to where I was standing
And I hear more whispers behind me.
Close behind me,
Nagging at me,
Making me feel worthless.
I have to do something about this!
I go to my loved ones,
But where did they go?
I'm alone, all alone.
Can I save myself now?
I can try at least,
And maybe I'll succeed.

When I'm back in the same place the next day,
I hear them again.
The whispers,

The horrible, nagging whispers.
But I won't let them bring me down this time,
Because I am strong.
I walk away,
But the whispers follow me.
I wasn't expecting this!
I thought they stayed,
Letting themselves float away into the wind,
Not caring about a soul.
But I was wrong!
I have to stay strong.
But it's hard, so hard.
Can I do this any longer?
Suddenly,
In the blink of an eye,
They fade away.
I see a figure walking towards me.
I'm scared at first, but its presence is reassuring.
It rests a hand on my shoulder
As if it was saying,
"You got this."

And now I'm back there again,
Standing.
That figure gave me hope.
I'll do it this time!
I hear them again.
I've done this for too long,
And it's time for it to stop.
For them to stop bringing me down,
Hurting me,
Nagging me.
I walk away,

And I can still hear them.
I feel the figure's presence again
And now I feel stronger.
I'm not alone,
I'm surrounded by people who love me.
I'm not afraid,
I'm strong.
The whispers slowly fade away,
And I look back at the figure.
I start to see it in more detail.
Short brown hair,
Deep brown eyes,
And a warm smile.
It's me.
I smile back.
I wasn't alone.
I always had someone with me.
Myself.
My beautiful self.

The Monster Inside My Head

Emma was asked to give a speech in front of the whole school. She was honored to be recognized for her academic achievements. She had practiced her speech in front of her mirror at least a hundred times. Right as she began walking up to the stage, I picked the lock on the vault she tried to put me in. I leaked every bad memory of public speaking like a sponge that couldn't hold any more water.

I'm the one who makes her overthink everything. *What if I stutter? What if my class laughs at me?*

I am the little nobody in her head with a very convincing voice. I come out when I'm not wanted. I want to help Emma by making her cautious, and trying to keep her safe, but sometimes I don't know when to leave. So, I never do. I stick by her side even when she tries to push me away.

She is stronger than me, yet she lets my quiet voice hold her back. *They're going to laugh at us. Why did we even say yes to doing this?*

She was once asked where the scariest place in the world is and responded with *"my head."* I don't let Emma accept anyone in her life. I think that if she lets them in it will cause her more pain than I have.

I am the one who makes her feel as though she is alone even when she is in a room full of people. *If I mess up my speech, who would even consider talking to me?*

Everyone has someone living inside their head. Everyone is supposed to have more than one voice living with them. You know, the ones that hype you up or make you cautious. Emma doesn't. All Emma has is me and a brain full of amazing ideas that I don't want her to share for I am worried that she will be rejected or hurt by someone. *They really aren't that bad are they? Who am I kidding? They are that bad.*

At irregular times I go through all the things she has done in a day and pinpoint the smallest things and make them major until they are eating away at both of our insides. *Is my outfit okay? I knew I should have gone with a nice sweater instead of a dress. I'm way too overdressed. I can't do this. There is no way I can do this.*

I am the one who ruins everything and holds her back. I am the monster inside her head; I am anxiety.

Tick Tock

Perpetual:
never ending,
never changing.

I watch,
your hands move with the second
Tick
You look at me,
I look at you,
You look   fragile,
like an old man
Tock

Time

The only constant in this world,
never ending,
never changing.
Tick
Your arms may stop,
but time,
it never will.
Tock

Time

Passively,
you watch.
The old man will age,
saying his last goodbye.
Tick
The child will no longer be a child anymore.
Tock

Time

I will never escape you.
afraid,
afraid of the future,
afraid of leaving this Earth,
of a last goodbye.

Time

Tick
I can't stop you,
for you hold time
in your arms.
Tock

Falling Deeply Into America - Խորապես ընկնելով Ամերիկա

Your words in my mouth flattened my tongue and stained like
coins that rusted onto my gums in
Their metallic twang
And then when finally I could choke them back their sliced
fragments echoed the dicing of dimes
That I heard ch-chang every time we'd cross a road in Midtown,
Your purple-flowered pinned purse clutched beneath the Good-
will flannel and
Even tighter your right hand clutching mine
Saying what I couldn't and probably wouldn't say
Whispering back
Putting the honks and the screams and the city scum to sedated
slumber
Whispering back from the receding yew you
Embroidered on Papik's work socks
The same whispering back Noah heard from high on Ararat
As voch'kharner welcomed him, grazing,
The same whispering you heard your own tatik
Soothe over you
Like a halo you were crowned
Gleaming still in those lonely nights huddled in hiding base-
ments damp
The same whispering I stuttered into
Ch-Chang-ing coins that clatter still
While your right hand clutches mine still
Խորապես ընկնելով Ամերիկա

I know I never paid much attention to you while you were around,
But at eight years old
When school resumed in early January
And Kate Jacob and Charlie all rambled
On of new shoes and dolls and stuffed bears
I only could mention how you always prayed with your hands facing down
As if somehow the cracks in your hands aligned with mine
And said what our mouths couldn't
In our gnarled embrace all down that road in Midtown
And I just knew you knew of a time
Vacant of God
A plane vacant of God
Where the winded sand whipped before settling on the bodies
That heaped into
The slabs where shadows once stood
That heaped into
Bodies of little ant hills rolling on the plane
Vacant of God
And I just knew you knew of a time
Where you'd sit by a window silly
And think if you held your hands up just high enough
Those cracks could ride onto the corner of the
Sky with you and expand
Like the silhouette of a t'rrch'un on the horizon,
With wings wide enough to withstand you and Tatik, Papik,
Mayrik, Hayrik, Anahid, and Arax
And feathers to fix all your fears with their float
And soft songs to steady you from the sights
Of lonely nights huddled in hiding basements damp.
If I had turned to you on Midtown

If I had braced through the metallic twang of words that
Flattened my tongue and stained like coins that rusted onto my
gums
Or if my own cracks in my own hands
In our gnarled embrace
Could repeat the same
Whispering back
The same whispering back Noah heard from high on Ararat
As voch'kharner welcomed him, grazing,
I would whisper back to you
Like the secluded halo you were crowned
And ask you
If one graveyard is better than the other.
Խորապես ընկնելով Ամերիկա
Խորապես ընկնելով Ամերիկա

You

The one thought that resembled coherence and juggled stability for my impulsive flight that night was this: that one day, I'd have to explain everything to you. My neglect. My dismissal. What I had done, why I did it, and why that night. And most importantly, how it felt.

I'm shaky, admitting it took me ten years. Mom, it was Christmas Eve. We all arrived at our house for dinner. No Bing Crosby or popcorn strings, just our hushed small talk around the table. It wasn't surreal, yet I couldn't offer the truth to your parents or "Baby Rue"… who is the first "baby" to ever be in middle school.

"No, Grandma, I'm just tired from the flight."
"I'm good, Rue, the eye bags are from studying."
"You know, I haven't been sleeping. Classic college."

Dad tries to make it feel like Christmas, but he can't capture the spirit like you did. Your straight-stitch stockings are above the fire, but your intoxicating gingerbread scent is missing. You'd waft it through the house, smiling, knowing our mouths were pooling at the edges. I can see you counting down the minutes, knowing like a mother does that Rue and I would come chasing, exploding into the kitchen. Then you'd just wink and say, "After dinner," while sneaking us the cookie dough you spared.

There is one piece you would melt over—a new ornament Dad made. A mahogany crafted miniature piano, like the one we used to play. A sanded, classy top, four swivelled legs, and perfectly blanketed white keys that glisten under the colored lights. But I don't touch it; it's always Rue, Dad, Grandma, or Grandpa that hangs it. Tradition was stabbed with delicate circles of gazes and floating nods between a broken family. In his planned manner, Dad choked, "Henry, would you like to hang it this year? For Mom?"

I had been running for ten years, not in a tangled maze or woods, but on a sidewalk, in a busy city. It looked like I was peacefully jogging, but I was running for the only life I've ever known, the one I needed to keep. Now I was met with this ugly reflection, pervading behind me in a store window. Bursting, like a million flames, I rushed as far as I could from the scene. Fists clenching the staircase, I pulled myself to the attic. Away from our once whole family and the ornament of your favorite instrument. There was unfinished business between us.

I had unveiled it; the white cloth flew, as if in slow motion. Dust flew like dandelions into the static air, as snow whirls in a snow globe. The dead walls inhaled, and the room waited in a newfound anticipation... The image, its flames ever growing, the painful resident of my mind, had morphed into a smoke, and I was high on it. It was revealed. Our Grand Piano, standing tall in the desolate state, had the courage after my abandonment. Standing triumphant and proud in my neglect, it was posed with grace and care in my hardened presence. I took it in fearfully, processing my now most hated treasure I would die to defend. My unworthy steps circled its field, and my dirty hand swept the surface. Dust blew off as if it became the Sahara, and the capsule was unearthed. The whites gleamed through our smudged fingerprints, like it was a portal back in time.

I hadn't told you, the first day of our ending as I drove us to the doctor, that I was terrified. That through anxiety-ridden Googling, I memorized more than a medical student. That my heart went still when I heard Dad downstairs whisper hello to the phone, that my head collapsed to the floor with my ear squeezed against the planks to hear what would follow, and that I was met only with my gasping for breath, a second before I sensed his complete loss for a response. We were now survivors at sea, no land in sight and no floatation, only constant beating against the waves. I felt that water rush between us during every hug, that sensation of two wet bodies clinging. Desperate for warmth, for life, for survival, and never quite knowing which wave was our last.

That water flooded through me then, and I striked the instrument. Chords reverberated like ribbons unravelling down a wedding aisle, each note like bells. My fingers nestled in their old spots as if the keys were mittens, and their ivory felt like your fingertips as you squeezed my hand from the hospital bed. Without warning or any divine sign leading up to this, the water flooded differently this time: it brought me back to you. The piano had always been the moon that hung over us night after night at sea. Now that I was playing it, with you nearby, it kissed the tide we once waded in and caressed the shore we had dreamed of. I was no longer afraid.

Prose/1ˢᵗ Place *Ealleannore VanNortrick*

10ᵗʰ Grade Concord Academy Petoskey

Moons Captivated by the Amber

I hear the crisp autumn leaves crunch under my paws. As I dart through the trees in the woods, the brisk air ruffles through my fur, and I can tell Winter is just around the bend. If only it wouldn't come so soon. The river rushes by my side, churning and bubbling, cold water spraying on my snout. Reaching the mouth, it calms down more while fish swim and sway through the water like the leaves flutter in the wind. Seeing myself in a rippled, glass-like form is a strange sight. My wavy snout, jagged ears, and amber-colored eyes stare back at me. My long ears twitch when I hear the snapping of a twig behind me. Turning back, I see a strange creature standing on two legs. My mind races as I wonder why it has such strange fur, only covering its head. What is it that wraps around its body that's colored the same as pumpkins? What is the long stick, and why is it silver? I wonder why it seems to be pointing the rod at me. BANG! A loud shot echoes throughout the woods. BANG! Another shot. Something jabs me. Then another shot and another jab. Finally, I fall to the forest floor, leaves crunching under my limp body, but I don't feel pain at all. It's strange, though. When I tell my body to get up, not a single muscle moves. Panic rushes through my brain, and no matter how hard I try, I can't do a thing. Pain begins to form in my side and leg. I still can't move an inch, but the strange creature moves close to me. Its piercing gaze stares into my soul. Why did you want to hurt me? What did you do? But most of all, what happens now? Their eyes are as black as night as they consume my vision. My consciousness fades.

I wake to see bars surrounding me. I'm unsure as to where I am. I no longer see trees, nor do I hear wind or water. Everything seems foreign and new. What happened? Where am I? Those strange creatures surround me, and they all look like the one that hurt me. What do they want with me, though? I try to hide in the corner of my confinement, but it seems I can't escape from it. All I can do is sit and wait for my fate to be decided.

It feels as though it's been ages since I was taken captive. The creatures have me in a place with more people around. There are other wolves within the captivity, but I miss my pack. Azrael has one blue eye while the other is amber flecked with gold. Her fur is silvery-grey in most areas, with white shining through due to age. She and her pup, Achlys, have been here for a long time. Zoriel was the alpha of his pack, but after what he calls "hunters" came, he was taken captive. Just like the rest of us, he got shot with something. There are several others, but I don't know them very well. I'm unsure as to how long I may be here. The others say Baccia was here for the passing of over 100 moons. If only I had a way of telling my pack I'm alive. If only.

It has now been over 60 moons since I arrived here. I spend most days sleeping. Maybe if I can't get out of here, I can spend my days in the world of dreams. Most days, I dream of running through the woods. My fur rustling in the wind, twigs breaking under my paw, and hearing the water rush nearby. I dream of seeing my mor and my far, the ones who raised me from the time I was a pu. Everything I once knew seems so foreign to think about now. A world that I was familiar with no longer exists in my sight. One day, I hope to see them again. Fenrisúlfr will soon take my soul. When that happens, I know I will be reunited.

Walloon Writers Review Eighth Edition Contributors

Kate Allore spends most of her free time either wandering the forests and beaches of Northern Michigan, or pondering these same places and the Beings that live there. She has been playing with words for a few years now as a way to sort out thoughts about the world and her place in it—hoping to give something beautiful back in return.

Elizabeth J. Bates: "I reside in the UP, which provides ample opportunity for photography. My photos have graced the covers of two publications besides the *Walloon Writers Review*: *Maiden Voyage* and *Stand Still in the Light*."

Milton J. Bates is the author of books about Wallace Stevens, the Vietnam War, and the Bark River watershed in Wisconsin. His poetry includes the collection *Stand Still in the Light (2019)* and two poetry chapbooks, *Always on Fire (2016)* and *As They Were (2018)*. He lives in Marquette, Michigan.

Suzi Banks Baum dwells at the crossroad of literary and visual arts. A writer, mixed media, and book artist, she teaches daily creative practice for writers, artists, and creative thinkers. Suzi's award-winning writing can be found in *The Good Life Review* and *Hypertext Magazine*. Raised in the Upper Peninsula of Michigan, Suzi lives in the Berkshires of Western Massachusetts.

James Bogan a professor of art history, a poet, and a film-maker, taught at the Missouri University of Science and Technology in Rolla from 1969 until 2012, at which point he was emeritized. His poetry and prose have been featured on National Public Radio numerous times. Scholarly publications include *Sparks of Fire* (1982) and *Bound* *to Belem* (2011). *Seven Wonders of Mackinac and Other Amazements* was published in 2018. He continues to write on occasion and to tend creeks in the Ozarks and brooks on Mackinac Island.

Monique Bova lives in a cottage on the edge of the Pigeon River State Forest, where she enjoys swamp tromping, bushwhacking, backpacking, and hunting for caddis larvae and antler sheds. The rich forests and beaver bottoms of northern Michigan provide most of her writing fodder.

Tom Conlan's prose and poetry have appeared in literary journals around the country, including *Michigan Trout Magazine*. His epic novel *Gentle Spirits* will be released in May 2023 from Legacy Book Press. For more information, including signed copies of Tom's work, please visit: www.thomasfordconlan.com

COVID prompted **Art Curtis** to begin work on *Letters to Harrison*, 53 letters to Michigan poet and novelist Jim Harrison, expected out in 2024. Three of the letters appear in *UP Reader #7*. Art's poetry has been published in *Walloon Writers Review*, *Peninsula Poets*, *Dunes Review*, and *TADL: Poets' Night Out*.

Mono D'Angelo publishing credits include: *Powers of Fate, Escape from a parallel Universe*, a poetry chap book, *Detroit News, Detroit Free Press, Sail Magazine, Trips and Journeys Magazine*, and multiple poetry publication. Mono is the past President of Poetry Society of Michigan and Director of Poets and Playwrights literary group. He has raced sailboats for 50+ years.

Dan Dueweke is a US Forest Service certified crosscut sawyer, axe and saw instructor, and saw filer who maintains trails for both the Little Traverse Conservancy and the North Country Trail Association. He resides in Charlevoix with his wife Janet Kohler, whose family has lived in the area since 1890.

Linda Nemec Foster is the author of twelve collections of poetry including *The Blue Divide*, *The Lake Michigan Mermaid* (2019 Michigan Notable Book), and *Talking Diamonds*. Her new book, *Bone Country*, is her first full-length collection of prose poems. The inaugural poet laureate of Grand Rapids (2003–05), Foster is the founder of the Contemporary Writers Series at Aquinas College.

Hailey French is a floral designer and artist in northern Michigan. She is constantly inspired by the Michigan landscapes and lakes around her. Her favorite mornings are spent drinking coffee with her partner Mike and cats, Millie and Clyde.

CJ Giroux teaches in the English Department at Saginaw Valley State University, and he is on the staff of Dunes Review. His most recent chapbook is *Sheltered in Place*.

Katie Gray developed a love for plants while spending hours exploring all the plant species growing in her parent's backyard. She went on to earn a B.S. in plant biology and currently works for a local conservation organization. In her free time, she enjoys photographing under-appreciated native plants to share their beauty and ecology importance with others.

Sheri Greene is a writer and jewelry and ceramic artist who resides in Grand Haven, Michigan. She is also a retired English and visual arts teacher with an M.F.A. in ceramics. Beyond her creative pursuits, Sheri cherishes time with her family as well as enjoys showing and training her horse, Swivel, and her dog, Lana.

Isabella Gross is a poet and artist. She is in her final semester in Miami University's MFA program. Her thesis is a collection of persona poems that gives voices to the voiceless, including the perspectives of northern Michigan landscapes, her maternal grandmother, and a Mars exploratory robot that focuses on renegotiating relationships in response to time and changing purpose.

Caroline Helmstadt is a writer and nature photographer from the Great Lakes Bay region. She most enjoys spending her time outside with her partner, Julien, who encourages her work; in their outdoor recreation, Caroline finds inspiration to explore the natural world in writing and images.

Betsy Hayhow Hemming enjoyed a varied career and has returned to her roots as a writer. She crafts columns and essays about northern Michigan as well as short stories. She self-published her first novel, *William Bell,* and now is working on a sequel. www.betsyhemming.com.

Steve Hooper is a writer, musician, and lover of all things Michigan and outdoors. He writes and performs music as Under This Cold Sky and hosts an Upper Peninsula and outdoors-themed podcast, *Saturday Sauna Night.* Steve is a lifelong Yooper and resides in the Marquette area with his family.

Deda Kavanagh lives in Bay City, Michigan. Her poems have previously been published in *Walloon Writers Review* and *Still Life 2020.* She is currently studying haiku, senryu,
and other short forms of poetry.

Taylor Keiser: "Being born and raised in Emmett County, Michigan and receiving my BA in Zoology at Northern Michigan University, I've always been an outdoor lover. In my free time I enjoy paddle boarding, kayaking, foraging, hiking, stargazing, and photography, all the while letting myself get lost in the wonder and curiosity of nature."

Kelly Suzanne Kelley: "I grew up in Southern California, but Michigan is truly my happy place! I've been living here for 20 years, and it is the most beautiful place I've ever lived."

Elizabeth Kerlikowske's latest chapbook is *The Vaudeville Horse (Etchings Press 2022)*. She is active with Kalamazoo's Friends of Poetry and the Poetry Society of Michigan and past president of both.

Bridget Klaasen lives in Suttons Bay with the best husband she ever had and the worst dog (or the other way around, it is sometimes hard to tell). She has been well mentored through the lifelong learning program at Interlochen Center for the Arts and appreciates this opportunity to meet new writers.

Katy Klimczuk is the author of *M is for Mackinac: A Nature Alphabet* (2023). She homeschools her children and lives in Grosse Pointe Farms, Michigan with her husband, two children, and two cats. Find out more at www.katyklimczuk.com.

Gloria Klinger lives in West Michigan where she enjoys walking the dunes and listening to nature. Her poems have been recognized on buses in Muskegon, and in competitions like the National Federation of State Poetry Societies, Art Prize, and Art Talks Back at Muskegon Museum of Art.

Katie Koziara earned her M.A. in fiction writing at Johns Hopkins University and her B.A. at the University of Michigan, where she studied at the Ford School of Public Policy and the Sweetland Center for Writing. She grew up in Northern Michigan and now lives in Washington, D.C.

James Lenfestey is an award-winning writer for his significant contributions to the Minnesota literary community. For fifteen years he chaired the Literary Witnesses poetry program in Minneapolis and led a summer poetry series on Mackinac Island, Michigan. He lives in Minneapolis and on Mackinac Island with his wife. They have four children and eight grandchildren.

Jeanne Blum Lesinski has deep roots to Cheybogan County, where the more than 100-year-old family homestead still stands. Her poems and poetry hybrids have appeared in many journals, including *The Dunes Review* and *The Ekphrastic Review*. Her poetry collection *Tethers End* is forthcoming from Shanti Arts. When not writing, she enjoys biking, birding, and photography.

Ellen Lord is a Michigan native. Her writing has appeared in *Dunes Review, Walloon Writers Review, U.P. Reader, R.k.v.r.y Quarterly Literary Journal, Peninsula Poets, TDAL/PNO* chapbooks, and elsewhere. She has won the Landmark Books Haiku Contest. She wishes to thank her fellow writers from Freshwater Poets and Charlevoices for their laughter and wisdom.

Raymond Luczak is the author and editor of more than 30 books. Recent titles include *Chlorophyll: Poems about Michigan's Upper Peninsula* (Modern History Press) and *once upon a twin: poems* (Gallaudet University Press), a Top Ten U.P. Notable Book of the Year for 2021. His next title is *Far from Atlantis: Poems* (Gallaudet University Press). An inaugural Zoeglossia Poetry Fellow, he lives in Minneapolis, Minnesota.

Paul Maxbauer, a retired history teacher, lives in Traverse City, Michigan, and writes poems and stories. His work has been selected for the PNO chapbook by Traverse Area District Library and has also appeared in *Dunes Review* and *Walloon Writers Review*.

Karen Nemecek is a retired public school teacher, theater buff, and a loud and proud Spartan football fan. Her poetry has appeared in *Beneath* *the Lilac Canopy* and the *Petoskey News-Review*. She lives in Petoskey and Higgins Lake with her husband and their aged basset hound.

Doug Pfaff is a writer, photographer, and frustrated fly fisherman. He currently helps host the award-winning "Stacking Benjamins" podcast and lives with his wife and two dogs on a small lake south of Charlevoix. He's been exploring northern Michigan most of his life.

Jeremy Proehl lives in Alpena, MI with his wife and two Labradors where they enjoy time in the woods. He works in the garage door industry but has been writing poetry for almost 20 years. His poems have been published both in print and online in many journals as well as in several anthologies.

Greg Rappleye's poems have appeared in *POETRY, The Southern Review, The North American Review,* and many other journals. His collection, *A Path Between Houses* (University of Wisconsin Press, 2000) won the Brittingham Prize and his book, *Figured Dark* (University of Arkansas Press, 2007), won the Arkansas Prize in Poetry and in the Miller Williams Poetry Series. Recent publications include *Tropical Landscape with Ten Hummingbirds* (Dos Madres Press, 2018). He teaches at Hope College, Holland, Michigan.

F.W. "Skip" Renker's poems have appeared in *Awakenings Review, Leaping Clear, Presence,* and many other publications, as well as the *Atlanta Review* and *Passages North* anthologies. His books are *Sifting the Visible* (Mayapple Press), *Bearing the Cast* (Saint Julian Press), and *A Patient Hunger* (Atmosphere Press). Skip's a graduate of Notre Dame and Duke and has an MFA from Seattle Pacific University.

Jennifer Uehlein Reynolds is a retired public school teacher who enjoys creative writing, photography, and exploring Michigan by way of water and woods. She and her husband Geoff live in Charlevoix.

Philip Rice is a composer and poet living on Mackinac Island where he serves as Program Director for Mackinac Arts Council and sits on boards of the Upper Peninsula Arts and Culture Alliance, Straits Pride, and the Upper Peninsula Poet Laureate Foundation. He has self-published two chapbooks.

Carol Ritter is a resident of Grand Traverse County, where she writes about, paints, and photographs the natural beauty of Northern Michigan. She has authored numerous business articles and international film reviews but now enjoys focusing her poetry and prose upon the flora, fauna, and topography of the wilderness.

Katherine Roth is the author of the chapbook *Unforgotten* and the memoir *The Good Fight: A Story of Survival, Love and Cancer* written with her husband, Greg Holmes. Her poetry has been published in *Peninsular Poets*, *Open Palm*, and *WildRoot Journal*. She lives in Traverse City and the high desert of Taos, New Mexico.

Kim Ruley: "I have been making images for as long as I can remember—my first camera was a Kodak 110 MickeyMatic around age six—which eventually led to pursuing a bachelor's degree in photography at Northern Michigan University. My philosophy is simple: The image is either there or it isn't, and exploration and utilizing available light are key to that philosophy."

David James "DJ" Savarese is a multi-genre writer who has authored *Swoon (2022)*, *A Doorknob for the Eye (2017)*, and has co-authored *Studies in Brotherly Love (2021)*. An Iowa Arts Fellow, he teaches poetry writing for the Lynx Project (Chicago) and co-produced and narrated the Peabody award-winning, Emmy-nominated documentary *Deej: Inclusion Shouldn't Be a Lottery (2017)*.

Ralph James Savarese is the author or co-author of six books and the co-editor of four collections. His creative work has appeared in *American Poetry Review*, *Bellingham Review*, *Brevity*, *New England Review*, *Ploughshares*, *Poetry International*, Salon.com, and many more. He lives in Iowa City, IA and spends a part of each summer in Wildwood Harbor on Walloon.

Gary Merrill Schils taught theatre and dance at Concord Academy Petoskey for twenty years. Currently he is the percussionists for Boundary Water Trio with Stephanie Cope and Bill Wilson. Gary's wife, Sylvia Jania, is a retired modern dancer and now plays banjo. They live in a restored hundred-year-old farmhouse north of Harbor Springs.

Moon Seagren lives in Petoskey, Michigan. Her photos were published in the *2022 Walloon Writers Review*. As a hobby, Moon enjoys photographing the natural beauty of Northern Michigan.

Melissa Seitz is a writer and photographer who lives with her husband in Higgins Lake, Michigan. Her work has appeared in *After: Stories About Loss & What Comes Next*, *The Bear River Review*, *The Dunes Review*, *The Lake*, *Walloon Writers Review*, and others. As of 04/15/2023, she has photographed the sunrise 1,932 days in a row.

Becky Serrano: At the small farm she and her husband share in Cross Village, Becky enjoys reflecting on the sights, scents, and sounds of God's Country—Northern Michigan—as well as life's adventures and challenges. Through writing she explores joy, wonder, humor, hurt, and healing. Capturing moments or processing emotion with words is both deeply personal and a privilege to share.

Michael Sipkoski lives in northwest Michigan and has been connected to Michigan's forests, cold waters, and remote areas, as well as its creative and cultural environment, throughout his life. The seasons and landscape are inspiring. His photographs and writing have appeared in *The Boardman Review* and *Michigan Trout*.

K. Matthew Springfield was born and raised in Michigan, and currently resides in Clawson. He views every trip he takes afield as an opportunity to learn something new and believes that the outdoors is for everyone. He can be found most weekends exploring his home state's lesser-known public lands and waters.

Edd Tury is a Michigan native and lives in Charlevoix County. Edd is an avid transcendentalist and enjoys forest bathing in unpeopled spaces. His writing has appeared in *Dunes Review, Walloon Writers Review, Open Palm Print, TADL/PNO chapbooks, Detroit Metro Times, Michigan Woods n Waters,* and more. He is a founding member of Charlevoices Writers Group.

Robert Vivian's latest book is *All I Feel Is Rivers,* a collection of dervish essays. He fly fishes whenever possible in Northern Michigan, and when he can't, he dreams about it any way.

A Master Photographic Artist, **Karen Walker** has collected numerous awards for her outstanding photographic work. She is past president of Professional Photographers of Michigan, Jordan River Arts Council, and the East Jordan Chamber of Commerce and serves on several boards. Karen's work can be found on her website www.KarenWalkerStudio.com.

Lindsay Way is a facilitator and strategist whose work emphasizes increased connection and creativity. She uses writing, photography, and group processes to help teams and individuals find direction. She currently resides in Cincinnati, Ohio, and her heart will forever be with the woods and water of Michigan that raised her. Find her at www.lindsay-way.com.

Neil White is a retired lawyer and a resident of Tupelo, Mississippi, who has spent many summers at Walloon Lake. When he was 30 years old, he took a 10-week photography class and has been hooked ever since. The sailboat in the photograph is a 17 Meter class, unique to this lake. Neil raced his family's 17, number 6, in the late 1950s during the Walloon Yacht Club series.

Ellen Schettling Whitehead: "Nature has always been the catalyst that awakens my writing urge. I have been writing a haiku inspired by my photos every day for six years now. An avid hiker, I find the woods and waters of Michigan provide endless writing possibilities!"

Sara Wright finds joy in capturing beautiful Mackinac Island from a romantic and vibrant perspective. Living and working on Mackinac Island year-round provides endless inspiration for photographing the ever-changing landscape of the seasons.

Glen Young is writer, teacher, ski instructor, and kayak guide, and divides his time between
Mackinac Island and Petoskey. He is at work on a novel.

Greg Young: "I'm a wildlife, travel, and street art photographer based in southwest Michigan. When working my shots in post-production, I compose them tightly as if they are all portraits. I'm always looking for subjects that can appear light-hearted or entertaining."

Autumn Trek ©2023 Caroline Helmstadt